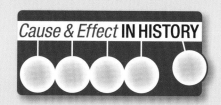

Cause & Effect IN HISTORY

Cause & Effect: World War II

John Allen

ReferencePoint Press®

San Diego, CA

About the Author

John Allen is a writer living in Oklahoma City.

© 2016 ReferencePoint Press, Inc.
Printed in the United States

For more information, contact:
ReferencePoint Press, Inc.
PO Box 27779
San Diego, CA 92198
www.ReferencePointPress.com

Picture Credits:
Cover: © Arthur Beaumont/National Geographic Society/Corbis; Maury Aaseng: 27; © Bettmann/Corbis: 35, 40, 43; Darren J. Bradley/Shutterstock.com: 7 (bottom, right); Depositphotos: 6; Everett Historical/Shutterstock.com: 7 (top), 24, 48; © Owen Franken/Corbis: 70; © Hulton-Deutsch Collection/Corbis: 20; S-F/Shutterstock.com: 7 (bottom, left); World History Archive/Newscom: 32, 60, 66; Neville Chamberlain (1869–1940) holding the Peace Accord, signed with Adolf Hitler (1889–1945) on 8th September, 1938 (b/w photo), English Photographer, (20th century)/Private Collection/Bridgeman Images: 10; The German infantry parade past Adolf Hitler on Ujazdowskie Avenue, Warsaw, 1939 (b/w photo), German Photographer, (20th century)/Private Collection/The Stapleton Collection/Bridgeman Images: 13; 'The Attack into the Unknown', German troops advancing on Stalingrad, from 'Signal', first edition of January 1942 (photo)./Private Collection/Bridgeman Images: 16; Operation Barbarossa, 1943 (color photo), German Photographer (20th Century)/© Galerie Bilderwelt/ Bridgeman Images: 51; Operation Barbarossa, 1941 (color photo), German Photographer (20th Century)/© Galerie Bilderwelt/ Bridgeman Images: 55

LIBRARY OF CONGRESS CATALOGING-IN-PUBLICATION DATA

Allen, John, 1957-
  Cause & effect : World War II / by John Allen.
    pages cm. -- (Cause & effect in history)
  Includes bibliographical references and index.
  Audience: Grade 9 to 12.
  ISBN-13: 978-1-60152-798-1 (hardback)
  ISBN-10: 1-60152-798-5 (hardback)
  1. World War, 1939-1945--Juvenile literature. I. Title. II. Title: World War II.
  D743.7.A428 2015
  940.53--dc23

                                                              2015016546

"History is a complex study of the many causes that have influenced happenings of the past and the complicated effects of those varied causes."

—William & Mary School of Education,
Center for Gifted Education

Understanding the causes and effects of historical events is rarely simple. The fall of Rome, for instance, had many causes. The onslaught of barbarians from the north, the weakening of Rome's economic and military foundations, and internal disunity are often cited as contributing to Rome's collapse. Yet even when historians generally agree on a primary cause (in this instance, the barbarian invasions) leading to a specific outcome (that is, Rome's fall), they also agree that other conditions at the time influenced the course of those events. Under different conditions, the effect might have been something else altogether.

The value of analyzing cause and effect in history, therefore, is not necessarily to identify a single cause for a singular event. The real value lies in gaining a greater understanding of history as a whole and being able to recognize the many factors that give shape and direction to historic events. As outlined by the National Center for History in the Schools at the University of California–Los Angeles, these factors include "the importance of the individual in history . . . the influence of ideas, human interests, and beliefs; and . . . the role of chance, the accidental and the irrational."

ReferencePoint's Cause & Effect in History series examines major historic events by focusing on specific causes and consequences. For instance, in *Cause & Effect: The French Revolution*, a chapter explores how inequality led to the revolution. And in *Cause & Effect: The American Revolution*, one chapter delves into this question: "How did assistance from France help the American cause?" Every book in the series includes thoughtful discussion of questions like these—supported by facts, examples, and a mix of fully documented primary and secondary source quotes. Each title also includes an overview of the event so that readers have a broad context for understanding the more detailed discussions of specific causes and their effects.

The value of such study is not limited to the classroom; it can also be applied to many areas of contemporary life. The ability to analyze and interpret history's causes and consequences is a form of critical thinking. Critical thinking is crucial in many professions, ranging from law enforcement to science. Critical thinking is also essential for developing an educated citizenry that fully understands the rights and obligations of living in a free society. The ability to sift through and analyze complex processes and events and identify their possible outcomes enables people in that society to make important decisions.

The *Cause & Effect in History* series has two primary goals. One is to help students think more critically about history and develop a true understanding of its complexities. The other is to help build a foundation for those students to become fully participating members of the society in which they live.

IMPORTANT EVENTS OF WORLD WAR II

1929
The stock market crash in the United States leads to economic turmoil and depression around the world.

1933
Hitler becomes chancellor of Germany and eliminates all opposition to the Nazi Party.

1925
Hitler publishes his book *Mein Kampf,* describing his program for restoring Germany after its defeat in World War I and its humiliation under the Treaty of Versailles.

1918
Germany is defeated by the Allies in World War I.

1910   1920   1930   1940

1935
Hitler deliberately violates the Treaty of Versailles by increasing the size of the German army.

1919
Germany signs the Treaty of Versailles under protest.

1940
Germany, Italy, and Japan sign the Tripartite Pact, forming an alliance against England and France.

1939
The Nazis and Soviets sign a nonaggression pact, setting the stage for the division of Poland between them.

1941
Japanese planes attack the US naval base at Pearl Harbor on the Hawaiian island of Oahu.

1946
Career American diplomat George F. Kennan outlines his idea of containment as the best way for the United States to counter Soviet aggression.

1943
German troops surrender at Stalingrad. The Soviet Red Army begins its own offensive, pursuing the Germans back across Europe.

1948
The United States and its allies respond to the Soviet blockade of Berlin with the Berlin Airlift.

| 1941 | 1943 | 1945 | 1947 | 1949 |

1942
US bombers sink four Japanese carriers, winning the Battle of Midway and turning the tide in the Pacific war.

1945
Nazi Germany surrenders on May 7, and Japan, after two atomic bomb attacks, surrenders on August 14.

1950
The United States enters the Korean War as part of a UN-led alliance against Communist North Korea, bringing the Cold War to Asia.

1944
American and French troops liberate Paris, France, from Nazi control.

Memories of Pearl Harbor

For Americans of a certain age, the Japanese attack on the US naval base at Pearl Harbor in 1941 was a defining event. All remember where they were on that Sunday morning in December when news of the attack hit the airwaves. Japanese bombers dropped a hail of torpedoes into the harbor, killing nearly twenty-four hundred people and sinking or damaging twenty-one ships and 323 military planes. The attack first shocked the nation, then brought a steely resolve to avenge what was viewed as an act of treachery. It took the United States four years to defeat Japan and its Axis allies, Nazi Germany and Fascist Italy. For the second time during the twentieth century, the United States entered a world war somewhat belatedly and helped lead the Allies to victory.

An Event That Shaped the Future

On December 7, 2014, seventy-three years after the attack, survivors gathered in Honolulu, Hawaii, to honor those who lost their lives at Pearl Harbor and share stories about the events of that awful day. The number of survivors dwindles with each passing year. In their Hawaiian shirts and military hats, many walking with canes or confined to wheelchairs, they suspect that this anniversary will one day be forgotten, like other landmark dates in history. "It's the same old story," says Jackson B. Davis, a former navy officer from Louisiana and survivor of the attack. "We don't hear much about Gettysburg anymore, or Bunker Hill. Or when the Normans took over England—we don't hear much about that."[1]

Nonetheless, the events of that day helped shape the succeeding decades. America responded to the attack by building the world's largest military force, defeating both Germany and Japan in World War II, and eventually becoming—after victory over the Soviet Union in the Cold War—the world's sole superpower. Today the United States enjoys friendly relations with the stable democracies in Japan and Germany. An American sailor scrambling for cover during the Pearl Harbor attack or a GI wading ashore at Normandy amid a storm of machine-gun fire might be forgiven for being skeptical about such an outcome. Yet the causes and effects that harden into reality often are the result of surprising decisions, unforeseen events, unintended consequences, and historical forces that come to light only years after the fact.

The Influence on Diplomacy and Politics

Events from World War II continue to influence how people view diplomacy and politics today. One example is the controversy over treaty negotiations regarding Iran's domestic nuclear energy program. Critics warn that the ruling mullahs in Iran are seeking to manufacture nuclear weapons that could vastly increase Iran's influence in the Middle East. They compare those in the West who believe an agreement with Iran will increase the chances for peace to Neville Chamberlain, Great Britain's prime minister from 1937 to 1940. It was Chamberlain who, in 1938, emerged from negotiations with Adolf Hitler holding aloft a signed treaty and proclaiming, "Peace for our time."[2] As political writer Joel B. Pollak contends,

> "It's the same old story. We don't hear much about Gettysburg anymore, or Bunker Hill."[1]
>
> —Jackson B. Davis, former US Navy officer and survivor of the Pearl Harbor attack.

> The reason Chamberlain's "peace in our time" is remembered is not that his theory of international relations was wrong but because he was hopelessly, dangerously naive about Hitler's intentions. A year after Chamberlain waved the paper on which he had signed the Munich Agreement, ceding the sovereignty of Czechoslovakia in return for Hitler's promises of peace, Germany had invaded Poland and Britain was at war.[3]

Thus, *Munich* is often invoked today as a shorthand term referring to the dangers of appeasement. In the same way *Pearl Harbor*—a disastrous episode in which Japan struck the US Pacific Fleet without warning—calls up the perils of not being prepared militarily for a sudden attack. Politicians and pundits often refer to these crucial events in drawing parallels to the current challenges faced by world leaders.

After meeting with Adolf Hitler in Munich in 1938, British prime minister Neville Chamberlain believed that allowing Germany to annex part of Czechoslovakia would delay further Nazi aggressions and lead to negotiations that would avoid another European war. He returned home to declare, "Peace for our time."

Historians still debate the causes and effects that shaped World War II and its aftermath. In considering the seeds of the war, for instance, they often cite the Treaty of Versailles, which imposed on Germany a harsh settlement that sparked a huge political reaction in that country and provided an opening for Hitler and his Nazi Party. Imperial Japan's decision to launch an attack on Pearl Harbor not only brought the United States into the war but also galvanized an unprecedented American military buildup. The timing of Hitler's decision to attack the Soviet Union left the German army faced with a war on two fronts that it finally could not win. Soviet leader Joseph Stalin's maneuvers to gain and secure territory at the war's end set the stage for a decades-long Cold War with the West. The effects of these events are still felt today across the globe. To understand current conflicts and crises in the world, it helps to examine the causes and effects of World War II.

The Allies Defeat the Axis Powers

World War II, which began in the late 1930s, grew out of the Great War (World War I) that took place two decades earlier. The Allies, which included Great Britain, France, Russia, Italy, and the United States, won victory over Germany and the Austro-Hungarian Empire in 1918. After the war, harsh terms imposed by the Treaty of Versailles left the German economy in shambles and its political system in disarray. Resentment over the treaty brought out strong feelings of nationalism among ordinary Germans. Extremist groups arose in the 1920s to take advantage of the people's impoverished state and desire for revenge. Among these was the National Socialist German Workers' Party, or Nazi Party. Leading the Nazis was a failed artist and malcontent named Adolf Hitler. He incited large crowds at Nazi gatherings with his impassioned speeches about gaining living space for the German people and punishing the supposed treachery of Jews, whom he blamed for Germany's defeat in World War I. In the early 1930s, with the world economy mired in the Great Depression, Germany began to emerge from its doldrums. In 1933 Hitler won election as chancellor of Germany and set about rebuilding its military and industrial might—despite restrictions on German rearmament in the Treaty of Versailles. Hitler also introduced laws and policies to strip German Jews of their citizenship rights and ability to earn a living.

Fascists, Militarists, and the War's Beginning

As Hitler seized power in Germany, dictatorships arose elsewhere in Europe and Asia that were bent on expansion by force. In Italy a journalist and soldier named Benito Mussolini led a Fascist movement based on socialism and nationalism and backed by paramilitary Black Shirt thugs. As dictator—or *Il Duce,* "the leader"—Mussolini subdued Libya and Somalia in the 1920s and conquered Ethiopia in the mid-1930s, establishing Italy as the dominant power from the western Mediterranean to the Red Sea. Mussolini rejected democracy with remarks such as, "The truth is that men are tired of liberty."[4] In Japan a right-wing nationalist regime gained power in the 1930s. Democracy in Japan gave way to military rule and virtual worship of the emperor, Hirohito. In 1931 Japanese armies occupied Manchuria in China and threatened further aggression in Southeast Asia. Japan's leaders spurned the United States and Western values that they perceived as being greedy and selfish.

"The truth is that men are tired of liberty."[4]

—Italian Fascist dictator Benito Mussolini.

Hitler embarked on his own series of conquests in Europe. In March 1938 Hitler's troops invaded Austria, enabling Germany to annex the country in a move called the *Anschluss*, or "union." In September British prime minister Neville Chamberlain tried to halt Hitler's aggression by agreeing to the Munich Pact, which gave Germany the Sudetenland, a region of ethnic Germans in Czechoslovakia. British crowds cheered Chamberlain's efforts to avert war, but some politicians were skeptical. "We seem to be very near the bleak choice between War and Shame," Winston Churchill, then a conservative member of Parliament, wrote to a friend in September 1938. "My feeling is that we shall choose Shame, and then have War thrown in a little later."[5] As Churchill feared, Hitler would not be appeased. A year later, on September 1, 1939, the German army swept into Poland. In response, Great Britain and France declared war on Germany. World War II had begun.

Also in 1939, impressed by Mussolini's triumph in Ethiopia and other battlefield successes, Hitler signed an alliance with Italy. In 1940 Germany, Italy, and Japan joined together in the Tripartite Pact, creating the alliance of the three so-called Axis powers. The terms of the agreement looked toward a new world order in Europe and Asia.

Blitzkrieg and the Battle of Britain

To avoid immediately fighting a war on two fronts, Hitler made another important move. He secured a mutual nonaggression pact with the Soviet Union, and he made a secret agreement with Stalin to divide Poland between them. This unleashed Hitler's armies to

Despite Hitler's assurances that he did not want war, his armies began their conquest of Europe in September 1939 by sweeping into Poland. Using blitzkrieg tactics, the German Army defeated the Polish defenders in roughly a month of fighting. A Nazi parade was held in Warsaw (pictured) to celebrate the victory.

rampage through Europe. They used a new style of warfare called blitzkrieg, or "lightning war." Germany attacked with overwhelming force and a combination of aircraft, infantry, tank divisions, and artillery. While the world looked on in horror, country after country fell to the German onslaught. Hitler redrew the map of Europe in less than a year.

Next, Hitler turned to the island nation of Great Britain. On July 10, 1940, the Luftwaffe, Germany's air force, began bombing raids over major British cities and military installations. Hitler planned to crush the British Royal Air Force (RAF) and prepare the way for a naval invasion of Great Britain. During the early weeks of the operation, more than two hundred German planes bombed London and other British cities every night—a strategy that Londoners dubbed the *Blitz* (short for *blitzkrieg*). Hitler's generals hoped to terrorize and demoralize the populace and force a quick surrender. RAF pilots fought back gamely, but British planes were

World War II and African Americans

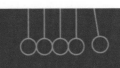

World War II brought new calls for an end to discrimination against African Americans. Early in 1941, even before the United States entered the conflict, 150,000 African Americans marched in Washington, DC, to protest discriminatory practices in the defense industry. President Franklin D. Roosevelt responded with an executive order outlawing such discrimination. Once war was declared, however, the US armed forces followed a policy of strict segregation. In the army, which had the greatest number of black troops, African Americans served in separate regiments headed by white officers. The Marine Corps had excluded blacks entirely before the war, and those who served in the Marines mostly worked in supply depots. The navy employed African Americans as cooks and servants, although some also had duties on gun crews. African American women volunteered for nursing or jobs in munitions factories, but they were also segregated. The Red Cross kept stores of blood plasma collected from African Americans separate from those for whites.

When given the opportunity, African Americans distinguished themselves in the war. The Tuskegee Airmen, a squadron of black pilots trained at Tuskegee, Alabama, skillfully flew escort fighter planes for bombers in North Africa, protecting them from attacks by enemy planes. Four of the Tuskegee pilots earned the Distinguished Flying Cross for their exploits. Yet discrimination in the armed services left African Americans even more determined to win social change. Membership in the National Association for the Advancement of Colored People grew tenfold during the war. Demands for racial justice would lead to the civil rights victories of the 1950s and 1960s.

outnumbered. Nevertheless, despite all the death, destruction, and piles of rubble, the British people refused to yield. Even the Nazis' use of incendiary bombs, which spread uncontrollable fires through city streets, failed to turn the tide. British antiaircraft guns began to have some success. The Luftwaffe, stretched too thin by fighting in Britain and in Eastern Europe, could not continue the nightly raids. By holding out against Hitler's onslaught, Great Britain won an improbable victory in what became known as the Battle of Britain. Historians point out that Britain was not as helpless as sometimes depicted. "Britain was the heart of a large, belligerent empire which was mobilizing rapidly in 1940 to confront the Axis threat," declares British war historian Richard Overy. "The support of Canada, Australia, New Zealand, South Africa, India and a string of colonies and protectorates made the [British] Empire a formidable foe. Fighter Command [the RAF] itself was a multinational force with crew from Europe, the Empire and the then neutral United States."[6] The United States, while technically neutral, also supported the British with the Lend-Lease Act. This program authorized President Franklin D. Roosevelt to transfer arms and supplies without compensation to countries deemed vital to US defense interests. With this support and a staunch will, Britain was able to deal Hitler his first defeat.

The War Widens

Despite this setback, Hitler was undaunted. He quickly reneged on his nonaggression pact with Stalin in order to pursue his main goal: conquest of the Soviet Union. On June 22, 1941, Germany and its allies launched a massive invasion of the Soviet Union. Operation Barbarossa, as it was called, stretched from the shores of the Baltic in the north to the Black Sea in the south. Surprisingly, considering Stalin's paranoia and distrustfulness, he did not expect Hitler's treachery—at least not so soon—and Russian troops were caught unawares by the attack. Initially the invasion met with great success. In September, emboldened by the death or capture of more than one hundred thousand Soviet troops at Smolensk, Hitler reckoned that the Red Army was on the brink of collapse and victory was within easy reach. Nazi forces swept eastward to the outskirts of Moscow by January 1942. But fatigue due to the huge distances covered, the harshness of the Russian winter, and the vast numbers of Soviet soldiers combined to stop the German advance. Hitler's plans for a triumphant parade through the streets of Moscow gave way to months of bloody fighting. Time and again the Red Army would retreat only to surge back with renewed determination. Operation Barbarossa settled into a vicious, grinding stalemate.

Hitler's brutal invasion of Eastern Europe and the Soviet Union was accompanied by a systematic effort to murder Jews, Poles, Roma (Gypsies), people with mental illnesses and physical disabilities, and others considered undesirable according to Nazi ideology. Mobile killing squads called Einsatzgruppen followed behind the invaders, round-

German troops and armor advance through the winter of 1941 toward Moscow. Blitzkrieg tactics coupled with the enemy's poorly led and disorganized forces allowed the German army to invade deep into the Soviet Union, bringing it to the gates of the Russian capital within four months.

ing up Jews in Polish towns and villages to be shot and dumped into mass graves. The Nazis also established concentration camps throughout the regions they occupied—camps that, by 1943, would be used to receive transported Jews and murder them by the thousands with poison gas.

At the end of 1941 US neutrality came to a sudden end. On December 7, 1941, Japanese planes attacked the US naval base at Pearl Harbor in Hawaii. Japan's leaders officially declared war on the United States only after the attack was under way. They hoped to cripple American naval forces in the Pacific and force the United States to accept Japanese supremacy in Pacific waters. The surprise attack failed, however, to deal the crushing blow Japanese strategists desired. The United States immediately declared war on Japan—and shortly thereafter on the other Axis powers. The American economy quickly changed to a war footing focused on manufacturing weapons and training hundreds of thousands of new troops. On April 18, 1942, US colonel Jimmy Doolittle led a bombing raid on Tokyo, the Japanese capital, and on the city of Nagoya. The raid had little military effect, but it served to boost American morale.

Less than a year after Pearl Harbor, American ground troops joined battle-hardened British forces to invade Algeria and Morocco in North Africa. Despite the tactical genius of Germany's field general Erwin Rommel, called "the Desert Fox" for his ability to strike at his enemy's weakest points, British forces overcame Rommel's army at El Alamein on the Egyptian coast. On November 10, 1942, British prime minister Winston Churchill expressed a cautious optimism about the triumph: "Now this is not the end. It is not the beginning of the end. But it is, perhaps, the end of the beginning."[7] In the ensuing months the Allies, led by two extraordinary commanders, British general Bernard Montgomery and American lieutenant general George S. Patton Jr., were able to encircle the Axis forces. The surrender of 230,000 Axis troops in Tunisia in May 1943 marked a major victory for the Allies.

The Tide Begins to Turn

Success in North Africa gave the Allies vital control over the Suez Canal in Egypt and strategic ports along the Mediterranean coast. They were able to employ North Africa as a base for the invasion of

Sicily and mainland Italy. In Sicily more than 140,000 Italian troops surrendered, leading Italy's Fascist Grand Council to remove Mussolini as Italy's leader in July 1943. Two months later the new Italian government secretly signed a peace agreement with the Allies. Allied invasion forces in Italy met resistance from German troops, and the Nazis were able to control northern Italy and reinstall Mussolini as a figurehead leader. Yet it took twenty-two German divisions to hold the Allied forces at bay. Churchill saw Italy as the so-called soft underbelly of Europe, the pathway to a wider invasion. American commanders George C. Marshall and Dwight D. Eisenhower, however, viewed Italy as a diversion from their true intent: invasion of Europe by crossing the English Channel into France.

Soviet leader Stalin, who had joined the Allies after Germany's assault on Russia, urged the Allied leaders to step up their invasion of Europe in order to relieve pressure on his own beleaguered armies. At the Battle of Stalingrad, German troops conducted a months-long siege from July 1942 to February 1943. They fought Red Army soldiers and civilian volunteers from street to street and building to building. Casualty numbers on both sides were devastating, with thousands dying each day. In November 1942 Soviet reinforcements were able to trap the German Sixth Army in a two-pronged pincer movement like the closing of enormous jaws. From that point, Soviet forces began to move rapidly westward, overcoming the Germans' counterattack. Nazi troops would now have to fight their way out of Russia and back across Eastern Europe. Hitler's dreams of conquest were laid to rest at the Battle of Stalingrad. The German people's morale collapsed. A secret opinion survey, taken in Germany by the Nazi intelligence service in February 1943, revealed the truth: "Fearing that an unfavorable end to the war is now possible, many compatriots are seriously thinking about the consequences of defeat."[8]

In the Pacific war, a major turning point occurred in June 1942 at the Battle of Midway. The Japanese lured the American fleet of aircraft carriers to the vicinity of the Midway Islands, located 1,300 miles (2,092 km) northwest of Honolulu. There, Admiral Isoroku Yamamoto planned to complete the job of destroying the US fleet that he had intended to accomplish at Pearl Harbor. Instead, American aircraft destroyed four Japanese carriers, losing only one of their own.

An End to Imperialism

One far-reaching effect of World War II was the blow it dealt to imperial powers like Great Britain and France. Britain's colonies provided vital resources needed for fighting the war, particularly oil from English possessions in the Middle East. Prime Minister Winston Churchill wanted to preserve the British Empire but realized it was more important to gain the support of the United States and its anti-imperialist leader, President Roosevelt. On August 14, 1941, Roosevelt and Churchill issued a joint declaration called the Atlantic Charter, one point of which was that people everywhere have the right to choose their own form of government. Ideas from the Atlantic Charter were incorporated into the declaration of the United Nations, making self-determination part of international law. Thus, while Nazi Germany and Imperial Japan were bent on subjugating nations, the Western Allies were acknowledging colonial peoples' right to freedom and an end to imperialism.

The enormous cost of waging war left the imperial powers weakened and scarcely able to administer their colonies. Postwar liberation movements arose in Africa, the Middle East, and Southeast Asia. But whereas Roosevelt opposed Western imperialism, he seemed less troubled by Soviet domination in Eastern Europe—or at least resigned to it. "[Roosevelt] frequently behaved as if Churchill's defense of his empire were a greater problem than Stalin's ambition to enlarge the Soviet sphere of dominance," writes historian Alonzo L. Hamby. Forty years would elapse before the nations of Eastern Europe achieved their own liberation from Soviet control.

Alonzo L. Hamby, "Dealing with Uncle Joe," *Wall Street Journal,* March 14, 2015. www.wsj.com.

The Pacific war would proceed in a series of desperate encounters over the next three years. Nonetheless, the Battle of Midway ended the notion of Japanese superiority at sea and in the air.

The D-Day Invasion

On June 6, 1944—known as D-day—Allied forces landed on the French coast of Normandy in the largest seaborne invasion in history. Allied soldiers slogged ashore from landing craft amid a hail of Nazi

American troops disembark on one of the Normandy beaches after fighting had moved inland. Operation Overlord, as the Allied invasion of the French coast was dubbed, proved a successful gamble that ultimately put US, British, Canadian, French, and Polish troops within striking distance of Germany.

gunfire. American air superiority and the coordination of landing troops enabled the Allies to establish a beachhead and slowly move inland. Military historian Craig L. Symonds points out that the landing on D-day was only the start of a massive operation:

> There is a tendency to conceive of the Allied landings on D-Day as a single event, but in fact it was just the first step. After seizing the beaches, the Allies then had to land hundreds of thousands of more men, vehicles, and equipment in a never ending stream that lasted for months, and they had to do it faster than the Germans could direct reinforcements to the

threatened area. Then, the Allies had to supply all those men with hundreds of tons of food, fuel, and ammunition, all of which came by sea.⁹

Combat proceeded across almost impenetrable hedgerows of trees in farmers' fields. Once past these barriers Allied troops pushed rapidly forward, with German forces in full retreat. With victory seemingly in their grasp, the Allies met with unexpected resistance as they neared the Rhine River and German territory. South of the Hurtgen Forest, Germany launched a surprise counterattack comprising a quarter-million troops and a thousand tanks. The assault, which began in December 1944, created a miles-wide bulge in the American lines, thus resulting in the battle's name—the Battle of the Bulge. American and British forces fought back to repel the onslaught, with huge losses of men and equipment. Nevertheless, Hitler's army was less able to absorb its own losses. Hitler himself committed suicide in a Berlin bunker on April 30, 1945. (Two days earlier Mussolini had been shot by Italian partisans and his body hung upside down at a gas station in Milan.) With American and British troops closing in from the west and Soviet troops from the east, Germany signed an unconditional surrender on May 8.

> "After seizing the beaches [at Normandy, France], the Allies then had to land hundreds of thousands of more men, vehicles, and equipment in a never ending stream that lasted for months, and they had to do it faster than the Germans could direct reinforcements to the threatened area."⁹
>
> —Military historian Craig L. Symonds.

Hiroshima, Nagasaki, and the War's End

In the Pacific, Allied forces—which were mostly American with additional troops from the British Commonwealth, including Australia and New Zealand—moved to capture a series of islands from the Japanese. The names of those islands would become storied in military lore: Guadalcanal, Tarawa, Iwo Jima, and Okinawa. Fighting became increasingly fierce and bloody as the Allies approached the Japanese homeland. Japanese military culture forbade surrender, so battles would continue to the last man. Mindful of the casualties that would be incurred in a final push toward Tokyo, President Harry S. Truman made the decision to drop the recently developed atomic bomb on the city of Hiroshima on August 6, 1945. Three days later, with the Japanese still refusing to surrender, another bomb fell on Nagasaki. On August 15 Japan formally surrendered, bringing to a close the deadliest war in history.

The grim statistics connected with World War II emerged over months and years. Deaths among the Axis powers, including military personnel and civilians, are estimated at 12 million, and the Allies suffered estimated losses of more than 60 million, including 42 million in the Soviet Union alone. Only later did the world learn the extent of the Holocaust, in which the Nazi regime murdered 6 million Jews and millions of other so-called undesirables. At war's end the United States and the Soviet Union stood unchallenged as twin superpowers. The effects of World War II would be felt to the end of the century. "Population centers that had mostly avoided the worst of the death and destruction continued to see poverty and hunger linger for years after the surrender documents had been signed," notes historian Kenneth T. Jackson. "Meanwhile, the prisoners and the wounded, making their way back to wives, sweethearts, parents, and children, often after an absence of many years, would carry the cost of the conflict with them for the rest of their lives."[10]

> "Population centers that had mostly avoided the worst of the death and destruction [in World War II] continued to see poverty and hunger linger for years after the surrender documents had been signed."[10]
>
> —Historian Kenneth T. Jackson.

How Did the Treaty of Versailles Contribute to Hitler's Rise?

Focus Questions

1. Why did the Fourteen Points, President Wilson's plan for the peace settlement after World War I, prove to be unrealistic?
2. Do you think the terms of the Treaty of Versailles were too harsh on Germany? Why or why not?
3. What part did the worldwide economic collapse of the late 1920s play in Hitler's rise to power?

On November 11, 1918, after four years of desperate warfare in Europe, Germany surrendered to the Allied powers, bringing to an end the so-called Great War. The armistice ended what was then the bloodiest war in history, with deaths of combatants and civilians approaching 9 million overall. It was the first war fought not only on land and sea but also in the air, and it encompassed not only officers and soldiers but also millions of civilians. A combination of modern weaponry and outmoded tactics had produced slaughter on the battlefield like nothing ever seen before. The appalling carnage seemed to demand some sort of revenge on those deemed to be responsible for starting the conflict. This was the mindset of many of the Allied diplomats as they shaped a treaty to bring the war to a formal end.

A Punishing Treaty

At the Paris Peace Conference, twenty-seven Allied nations took part in creating the treaty, but the main drivers of the process were the Big Four nations—Britain, France, Italy, and the belated entrant into the war, the United States. President Woodrow Wilson hoped to base the

Crowds in Times Square, New York, hold up newspaper headlines that declare "Germany Surrenders" after news of the armistice reached US shores. The destruction from what had been the bloodiest war ever left many politicians and citizens in all countries eager to avert another global conflict.

agreement for peace on his own Fourteen Points, a list of guiding principles for the postwar world that he had presented to a joint session of Congress on January 8, 1918. Wilson's Fourteen Points were aimed at correcting the conditions that had led to a worldwide conflict. "It will be our wish and purpose," Wilson announced to Congress, "that the processes of peace, when they are begun, shall be absolutely open and that they shall involve and permit henceforth no secret understandings of any kind."[11] Point One called for an end to the kind of secret treaties and alliances that were the work of Germany's nineteenth-century chancellor, Otto von Bismarck. It was these tangled agreements that had pulled nations into the war in the first place. Point

Two guaranteed free navigation of all seas. Point Three mandated an end to trade barriers between countries. Point Four demanded a reduction in armaments to the lowest possible level consistent with security concerns. Point Five called for changes to colonial claims based on the right of self-determination. Points Six through Thirteen dealt with specific postwar matters of territory. Point Fourteen advised that nations should join together in a group so that future conflicts could be settled peacefully through negotiation—the idea that led to the League of Nations.

However, Wilson's plan proved to be hopelessly naive with regard to the aims of the other members of the Big Four. Prime Minister Georges Clemenceau of France rejected Wilson's idealistic dreams of peace. The war had been fought mainly on French soil, and France had lost 1.4 million soldiers and had suffered massive damage to roads, telegraph lines, coal mines, and other assets necessary to daily life. The French leader sought not only to prevent Germany from mounting future attacks on his country but also to punish it harshly for its aggression. He wanted war reparations—large cash payments from Germany to the Allies—and trade sanctions. "Clemenceau was also determined to cripple German trade, so the treaty stipulated that Germany had to accept all imports from Allied countries," writes historian Stephen Clarke. "Clemenceau was furious that penknives engraved with 'La Victoire' [victory], on sale in France, had been made in Germany. The exports, he said, had to start flowing in the other direction."[12] British prime minister David Lloyd George was more sympathetic to Wilson's plan. He privately believed that if Germany became destitute from paying war reparations and losing trade, its government might fall prey to Communist revolution as in Russia. Yet Lloyd George feared the plan's effects on Britain's colonies and also was aware of the British public's demands to make Germany pay. Adding to the devastation in Europe—and the people's bleak perspective—was the outbreak of the Spanish flu in mid-1918,

> "It will be our wish and purpose that the processes of peace, when they are begun, shall be absolutely open and that they shall involve and permit henceforth no secret understandings of any kind."[11]
>
> —President Woodrow Wilson.

which killed 25 million. Overall, bitterness in Europe ran high, and few were willing to be lenient toward Germany and its allies.

Germany Signs in Protest

On May 7, 1919, the German delegation to the peace conference received the finished treaty. Further negotiation of its terms—or any further discussion—was not allowed. The Allies demanded that Germany either sign the document or face a resumption of war, this time with a badly depleted army. Expecting to be consulted on the final terms, the Germans reacted with outrage, yet they had no real choice in the matter.

Aside from creating the League of Nations, the final treaty bore little resemblance to Wilson's program for peace. The terms instead reflected Clemenceau's demands. Germany had to acknowledge its guilt in starting the war. Because of this responsibility, Germany was forced to pay reparations to the Allies, mainly to France and Belgium for damage done to the infrastructure in those countries, including roads, bridges, and telegraph lines. The amount required was not specified, basically giving the Allies a blank check to be cashed at their convenience. Territory was seized from Germany, including Alsace-Lorraine (given to France); West Prussia, Posen, and Upper Silesia (given to Poland); and the Sudetenland (incorporated into Czechoslovakia). The German economy was hamstrung with debt and with the loss of manufacturing and resources in the relinquished areas. Germany was also forbidden to unite with Austria to boost its economy. The treaty limited Germany's army to one hundred thousand soldiers and allowed it no tanks or aircraft.

The signing ceremony took place at the Palace of Versailles on June 28, 1919—the fifth anniversary of the assassination of Archduke Franz Ferdinand, the incident that had triggered the war, and now twice a fateful date for the future of Europe. To ensure that the reluctant Germans would sign, the Allies raised a naval blockade to limit supplies to an already weakened Germany. The German delegation—sent by a new chancellor after the angry resignation of his predecessor—signed the Treaty of Versailles under protest. Before the ink was dry, a satisfied Clemenceau slipped outside for a stroll in the palace gardens, murmuring, "It is a beautiful day."[13]

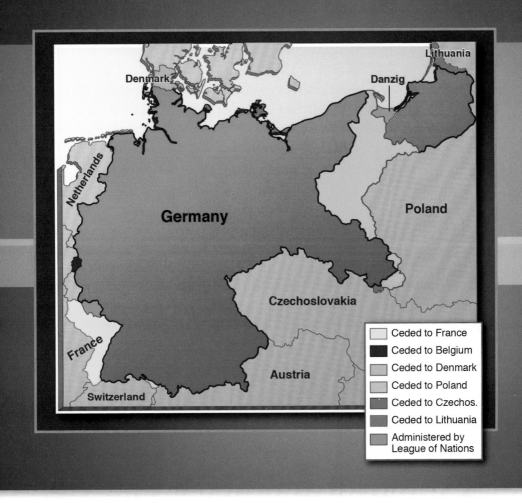

Reaction to the Treaty

The Treaty of Versailles was basically a public bankruptcy notice delivered to the nation of Germany. The final sum set for reparation payments eventually reached a staggering 226 billion marks, and the depleted German government began to default on its payments almost immediately. Ordinary Germans lashed out at the treaty's terms, particularly the assignment of guilt to Germany alone. They viewed the agreement as an attempt to humiliate their country. Those who signed the treaty were called the November Criminals (referring to the time of the original armistice), and foreign minister Herman Midler was labeled a traitor. The treaty drew criticism outside Germany as well. The British economist John Maynard Keynes, who represented the British Treasury at the peace talks, foresaw the damaging effects of the emerging treaty and resigned in protest. In his 1919 book *The Economic Consequences of the Peace,* Keynes declared, "If we aim at the impoverishment of Central Europe, vengeance, I dare say, will not limp. Nothing can then delay for very long the forces of Reaction and the despairing convulsions of Revolution, before which the horrors of the later German war will fade into nothing, and which will destroy, whoever is victor, the civilization and the progress of our generation."[14]

The US Senate also rejected the treaty, although for much different reasons. Senators deplored the fact that President Wilson had not consulted them on the agreement, and most were skeptical about the United States joining an international group like the League of Nations. The Senate's no vote basically spelled doom for the league, which needed American backing and membership to be effective. Although the League of Nations did form in 1919, it never became the agency for settling disputes among major powers that Wilson had envisioned. As Italian dictator Benito Mussolini was to put it, "The league is very well when sparrows shout, but no good at all when eagles fall out."[15]

> "If we aim at the impoverishment of Central Europe, vengeance, I dare say, will not limp. Nothing can then delay for very long the forces of Reaction and the despairing convulsions of Revolution."[14]
>
> —British economist John Maynard Keynes.

Germany's economy spiraled down into ruin during the 1920s. German businesses faced crushing tariffs in other countries that prevented them from selling their goods there and depressed the economy. With unemployment growing, the Weimar Republic—the democratic government that led Germany—tried to support workers with more spending on transportation projects and social programs. Added to these problems was the need to make stiff reparations payments as required in the Treaty of Versailles. This led the government to print incredible amounts of money, causing a state of hyperinflation. The German mark became almost worthless. Store shelves were often empty. Cartoons of the time showed Germans pushing wheelbarrows

At the end of World War I many Americans felt disillusioned with world affairs. President Wilson had overcome his nation's traditional isolationist attitude to lead it into a bloody conflict in Europe. Despite the US military's role in winning the war, Americans believed it was futile to get involved in European rivalries and hatreds that dated back centuries. Many had doubts about the commitments called for in Wilson's cherished idea of a League of Nations. Thus, having convinced negotiators in Europe to include the league in the Treaty of Versailles, President Wilson returned home to face an even more difficult job of persuasion.

In July 1919 Wilson, a Democrat, presented the treaty to a Republican-controlled Senate. Many hard-line Republicans refused to ratify an agreement that obligated the United States to come to the defense of other nations. Wilson, already weakened by cardiovascular disease and near exhaustion, decided to take his argument to the people. Against his doctor's orders, he set out on an 8,000-mile (12,875 km) railroad tour of the West, making more than thirty speeches along the way. In Pueblo, Colorado, Wilson collapsed and was rushed back to Washington, DC. On October 2 he suffered a massive stroke that left him paralyzed and barely clinging to life. Although Wilson survived, he had lost his strength. The Senate rejected the Treaty of Versailles outright. The United States returned to isolationism, making its role merely that of an anxious onlooker as Hitler seized power in the 1930s.

filled with cash in hopes of buying a loaf of bread. The Great Depression that struck the rest of the world in 1929 delivered a mortal blow to the German economy. Investors in the United States demanded repayment of short-term loans they had made to help Germany recover. Suffering increased among ordinary Germans, and the Weimar Republic tottered toward collapse.

Political Instability and the Rise of Hitler

Never widely popular among Germans, the Weimar Republic consisted of a coalition of smaller political parties that now began to fall apart.

Among the parties that vied to replace the Weimar government were Communists and Socialists on the left and Nationalists on the right. One party had established itself in Munich, the chief city in Bavaria and a center of resentment toward the Weimar Republic. The National Socialist German Workers' Party, often abbreviated as the Nazi Party, capitalized on people's anger about the weakness of the Weimar government and its supposed treachery in leading Germany to surrender and submit to a humiliating treaty. The leader of the Nazis was a former army corporal and failed artist named Adolf Hitler. Originally sent to spy on the party as a government agent in 1920, Hitler ended up joining the group and rising to a position of leadership. Hitler and the Nazis also made use of a paramilitary group in Munich called the Freikorps. Its members were German troops who refused to disarm after the war. Influenced by Mussolini's Fascist gangs of black-shirted henchmen, Hitler and Ernst Röhm, a Freikorps veteran, incorporated the troops into the Nazi Party as a private force of paramilitary thugs called the Brown Shirts or Storm Troopers. Employed for security at Nazi rallies, the Brown Shirts used violence to intimidate members of other political parties and anyone who opposed the Nazis. By 1930 their numbers had grown to exceed the troop limits laid out in the Treaty of Versailles.

As leader of the Nazi Party, Hitler took advantage of the general misery and panic brought about by the 1929 stock market crash and worldwide depression. In his mesmerizing speeches in front of large crowds, he repeatedly emphasized two ideas: that the Treaty of Versailles was a *diktat*—a dictated ultimatum designed to destroy Germany—and that shadowy figures in the Weimar Republic were responsible for the stab in the back that prevented Germany from winning the war. Hitler also railed against German Communists, whom he saw as a greater threat than the Weimar politicians. Linking these ideas was Hitler's virulent anti-Semitism, or hatred of Jews. On the one hand, he claimed that it was Jewish industrialists who had sold out Germany to the Allies at the end of the war. On the other, he pointed out that Marxism, the radical ideology followed by Communists, was the invention of a Jew, Karl Marx; drew its main support from Jews; and thus was another example of destructive Jewish influence.

Many Germans saw through these emotional appeals and assumed that their countrymen would soon grow weary of Hitler's outlandish tirades. But instead, his popularity only grew. Crowds of the jobless and downtrodden, looking for scapegoats to blame for their condition, roared in agreement when Hitler claimed that it was the Jews, the hated treaty, and devious foreigners who were destroying the nation. A few years before, while in prison for his role in a failed attempt to overthrow the Weimar government, Hitler had dwelt on how easily people could be fooled. In his memoir, *Mein Kampf,* he writes, "The size of the lie is a definite factor in causing it to be believed, for the vast masses of a nation are in the depths of their hearts more easily deceived than they are consciously and intentionally bad. The primitive simplicity of their minds renders them a more easy prey to a big

Hitler and the Treaty of Versailles

Hatred of the Treaty of Versailles shaped Hitler's strategy from the beginning. For Hitler, it stood as a constant affront to Germans. "Each point of that Treaty," he writes in *Mein Kampf,* "could have been engraved on the minds and hearts of the German people and burned into them until sixty million men and women would find their souls aflame with a feeling of rage and shame."

Once in power, Hitler set about to shred the Treaty of Versailles. In 1934 he pulled out of the Disarmament Conference in Geneva, Switzerland, claiming that Germany had been disarming for fourteen years. In 1935 he increased the German army to half a million soldiers, and he made a pact with Britain (which admitted the treaty's unfairness) that allowed for expansion of the German navy as well. Both of these moves were violations of the treaty. In 1936 Hitler sent German troops back into the Rhineland, another explicit violation. In 1938 he invaded Austria and forced that nation to accept the *Anschluss,* or "union." In 1939 he attacked Poland and set in motion a larger effort to acquire living space for the German people—again, a deliberate breach of the Versailles plan to limit German-controlled territory. It was as if Hitler had a list of the treaty's terms and was systematically crossing them off one by one. As British prime minister Winston Churchill insisted, Hitler's plans were easy to predict: one simply had to read his book.

Adolf Hitler, *Mein Kampf,* Mondo Politico. www.mondopolitico.com.

lie than a small one."[16] Hitler's big lies about the source of the German people's misery got results. In the 1930 election, the Nazis won the second-highest vote total among all parties.

Hitler and the Nazis Gain Power

Hitler continued to prey upon the people's emotions by hammering his message home. He promised to bring order to chaos and return the German nation, and particularly what he described as the ethnically pure Aryan race, to glory. He guaranteed jobs for the unemployed and profits to factory owners. He promised an array of social programs to

The Reichstag fire of February 1933 was blamed on an unemployed Dutch Communist. Adolf Hitler, the newly appointed chancellor of Germany, used the event to stir anti-Communist sentiment that quickly led to mass arrests of Communist Party members throughout the country.

combat poverty and an end to class distinctions. He vowed to shred the Treaty of Versailles, defeat the Communists, and show the Jews no mercy. In the presidential election of 1932, Hitler lost to the tired old war hero Paul von Hindenburg, but, with the Nazis' popularity growing, he was eventually installed as the new chancellor. Once Hitler took power, democracy in Germany quickly came to an end. In February 1933 Nazi Brown Shirts torched the Reichstag, the building that housed Germany's legislature. Hitler blamed the fire on Communists and used it as a pretext to smash the enemies of the Nazi Party. In short order Hitler began arming the nation in direct violation of the Treaty of Versailles. His Brown Shirts already numbered four times what the treaty allowed. He instituted new laws to strip Jews of their rights as citizens. As the economy revived, millions of Germans praised Hitler as the nation's savior. They were ready to follow his plans for conquest and expansion. "The Treaty of Versailles," observes German historian Wolfgang Mommsen, "created a political climate in Germany in which the right put all the blame on everything that went sour, onto the treaty and the lost war. And that created this climate in which many people then began to think one had to fight the war once again."[17]

> "The Treaty of Versailles created a political climate in Germany in which the right put all the blame on everything that went sour, onto the treaty and the lost war."[17]
>
> —German historian Wolfgang Mommsen.

How Did the Japanese Attack on Pearl Harbor Influence the War's Outcome?

Focus Questions

1. Was President Roosevelt more concerned about the threat to the United States from Japan or Nazi Germany? Explain your answer.
2. Why was the US Navy so ill-prepared for the attack on Pearl Harbor?
3. Do you think the outcome of the war would have been different if Japan had completely destroyed the US Pacific Fleet in the Pearl Harbor attack? Why or why not?

On September 27, 1940, ministers from Japan, Germany, and Italy signed the Tripartite Pact, cementing the military alliance of the Axis powers. Japan officially recognized Germany and Italy as the leaders of a new world order in Europe, just as Germany and Italy affirmed the same position for Japan in East Asia. The agreement pledged each of the parties to come to one another's aid if attacked by a power not already engaged in war. The hope was that the United States, still neutral at this point, would think twice before entering a conflict that would instantly become a war on two fronts. Thus, Germany would not face American reinforcements in its battle against Britain, and Japan would be free to extend its domination in Asia. President Franklin D. Roosevelt saw the limits of the US position: saddled with inadequate forces while potential enemies were gathering strength in Europe and Asia. "It is terribly important for the control of the Atlantic," he told his adviser Harold Ickes, "for us to keep peace in the Pacific. I simply have not got enough Navy to go around—and every little episode in the Pacific means fewer ships in the Atlantic."[18]

Japanese Expansion in the Pacific

Japan, like its new partners in the Tripartite Pact, was a growing military and industrial power seeking expansion. A lack of natural resources in the islands of Japan forced the government to seek elsewhere for the raw materials it needed, including in the East Asian and US markets. For example, most of Japan's oil and steel came from the United States, and most of its rubber came from British Malaya. Japan's leaders also resented what they viewed as unfairness in international trade. "Their attempts to integrate the Japanese economy into a liberal world order . . . became frustrated in the early 1930s when the depressed western economies placed barriers on Japanese trade to protect their own

Government officials from Germany, Japan, and Italy toast the signing of the Tripartite Pact in Berlin that cemented the Axis alliance. This mutual assistance pact was staged primarily as a propaganda tool because the Japanese army and its Western counterparts operated on opposites sides of the globe.

colonial markets," writes British historian Susan Townsend. "Many Japanese believed that the structure of international peace embodied in the League of Nations favored the western nations that controlled the world's resources."[19] As a result, Japan began to look at other ways to secure vital resources, by force if necessary.

Since its surprising victory over czarist Russia in 1905, Japan had proven its ability to adapt Western technology, military equipment, and tactics to its own tradition of *bushido,* or "way of the warrior." *Bushido* emphasized not only courage and indifference to pain but also unquestioned loyalty to the emperor, who was regarded as almost divine. The willingness of Japanese soldiers to sacrifice for their emperor, combined with production of state-of-the-art ships and aircraft, made Japan a formidable military force. As the military took increased control of the government, Japan became much like a totalitarian state, with economic decisions and plans for production made at the highest levels. Its leaders decided that to maintain strength as an industrial power Japan must expand its territory in East Asia. Using its superior forces, particularly its fleet of aircraft carriers and battleships in the Imperial Navy, Japan sought to overwhelm its foes with rapid strikes, much like the Nazis' blitzkrieg strategy. By the late 1930s it had expanded into Korea and Chinese Manchuria to acquire certain resources. In July 1941 Japan set its sights on Southeast Asia, hoping to seize oil fields in the Dutch East Indies, British-owned rubber plants in Malaya, and French-run tin mines in Indochina.

President Roosevelt had kept the Japan problem on the back burner as he focused on Germany's assault on Britain and America's lend-lease program to support the British. Roosevelt was concerned about Japanese expansion, particularly Japan's drive to occupy Chinese Manchuria and dominate Chinese markets by force—countering the US policy of open trade—and its aggression in Southeast Asia. A militaristic Japan grabbing territory in the Pacific was an alarming development. Roosevelt wanted to avoid war with Japan, telling

> "The [American] embargo shocked the Japanese and reminded them of their economic vulnerability. The action increased the power of [Japanese] hawks who called for dramatic action."[21]
>
> —American historian Steven M. Gillon.

Churchill it would be "the wrong war in the wrong ocean at the wrong time."[20] However, his policy of so-called moral embargo—urging US firms not to provide the Japanese with credit, raw materials, or plans for building aircraft—was no longer sufficient to deter Japanese aggression. Roosevelt hoped to send a warning to the Japanese militarists while still avoiding a full-blown confrontation. In July 1941 he ordered a freeze on all Japanese assets in the United States and demanded more-stringent rules for exports, intending to slow—but not cut off—shipments of American oil to Japan. However, bureaucratic confusion led to a complete embargo of all exports to Japan, including oil. The Japanese relied on outside sources for 90 percent of their oil. "The embargo shocked the Japanese and reminded them of their economic vulnerability," notes American historian Steven M. Gillon. "The action increased the power of [Japanese] hawks who called for dramatic action. One Japanese leader remarked that the nation was 'like a fish in a pond from which the water was gradually being drained away.'"[21] Japan now saw war with the United States as inevitable.

The Attack on Pearl Harbor

American leaders also recognized the increased likelihood of war with Japan. The US Pacific Fleet had been relocated from California to Pearl Harbor on the Hawaiian island of Oahu in June 1940. Roosevelt planned the move as a demonstration of American naval power and as a deterrent to Japanese aggression against US possessions in the Pacific, including Hawaii, Guam, and the Philippines, as well as British and Dutch colonies. However, the move also left the Pacific Fleet vulnerable to attack by the Japanese navy. By November 1941 American naval officers were convinced a Japanese attack would occur in the Philippines, which were closer to Japan, or against US bases at Wake Island and Midway. They viewed an attack on Pearl Harbor as unlikely for two main reasons: the waters in Pearl Harbor were too shallow for an airborne torpedo attack to be effective, and Pearl Harbor's great distance from Japan would surely enable the US Navy to detect the approach of a large Japanese carrier fleet. Army and navy commanders at Pearl Harbor interpreted a war warning issued by US Army chief of staff George C. Marshall as chiefly a precaution against sabotage

Immediately after the Pearl Harbor attack, calls for revenge against Japan rang out all over the United States. Reports about Japanese naval forces rampaging through Asia and the Pacific only added to Americans' anger and frustration. With its Pacific Fleet in ruins and its push to rearm just beginning to ramp up, the US military had few options available. Nevertheless, President Roosevelt realized that American morale needed a boost. He ordered senior US commanders to devise some kind of response against Japan.

The task was not easy. The US Army Air Forces lacked bases close enough to Japan to support a bombing mission. Finally, it was decided to launch medium-range B-25 bombers from an aircraft carrier in the Pacific. Lieutenant Colonel Jimmy Doolittle led the mission and its preparations. Doolittle requisitioned bombers and had them modified with extra fuel tanks for the long flight. On April 18, 1942, a rainy, blustery morning at sea, Doolittle and his fellow pilots took off from a carrier 650 nautical miles (1,204 km) from their targets in Japan. The sixteen planes flew single-file barely above the waves to avoid detection. By noon they were able to bomb military and industrial targets in Tokyo and other Japanese cities. Although the Doolittle Raid caused little serious damage, news reports of its success helped raise the spirits of the American public. The raid also provoked Japanese admiral Isoroku Yamamoto into an ill-conceived attack on Midway that resulted in a major defeat for the Imperial Navy.

by local Japanese immigrants. With this in mind, commanders kept ammunition at Pearl Harbor safely locked away rather than available for use. Likewise, US aircraft were grouped closely together on the airfields so they could be guarded more easily. Army P-40 fighter planes designed to intercept attacks by incoming aircraft were diverted to Wake and Midway. Pearl Harbor, while not defenseless, was poorly prepared for an attack.

In late November a huge Japanese strike force—including battleships, destroyers, submarines, and carriers bearing more than four hundred aircraft—set out for Pearl Harbor. Japan's vice admiral Chuichi Nagumo managed to synchronize the fleet's movement with an enormous weather front at sea. This, plus the use of radio silence, enabled the Japanese to approach undetected. On December 7, 1941, at 6:00 a.m. local time, Japanese planes began to attack, bombing the harbor and strafing the airfields. It was a devastating assault that destroyed the battleship *Arizona* and left seven other battleships severely damaged. Several cruisers and other vessels were wiped out, and more than three hundred aircraft were destroyed or damaged. Among American personnel there were 2,388 dead and 1,174 wounded. With one operation, the Japanese had crippled the US Pacific Fleet. The attack on Pearl Harbor was a success beyond anything the Japanese high command could have imagined.

An Unintended Sneak Attack

At the time of the Pearl Harbor attack, the United States and Japan were officially in the midst of talks that would end the US oil embargo. It was Japan's intention to break off the talks shortly before the attack began. However, Kichisaburo Nomura, the Japanese ambassador in Washington, DC, experienced delays in decoding and transcribing cabled instructions from Tokyo. By the time the ambassador delivered the message declaring an end to negotiations to US secretary of state Cordell Hull, Japanese planes had already been bombing Pearl Harbor for more than an hour. The result was to shift attention from the fact that American forces were unprepared to Japan's treachery in launching a sneak attack while peace between the two countries still prevailed. "I have never seen a document that was more crowded with infamous falsehoods and distortions," fumed Secretary Hull upon receiving Nomura's message, "on a scale so huge that I never imagined until today that any government on this planet was capable of uttering them."[22] Hull's outrage very quickly spread to the entire nation.

In preparing his remarks about the attack, President Roosevelt added a key word to the speech: *infamy*, meaning public knowledge of extreme evil. At 12:30 p.m. on December 8, Roosevelt addressed a joint session of Congress and one of the largest audiences in the history of radio:

Yesterday, December 7, 1941—a date which will live in infamy—the United States of America was suddenly and deliberately attacked by naval and air forces of the Empire of Japan. The United States was at peace with that nation and, at the solicitation of Japan, was still in conversation with its government and its emperor looking toward the maintenance of peace in the Pacific. . . . It will be recorded that the distance of Hawaii from Japan makes it obvious that the attack was deliberately planned many days or even weeks ago. During the intervening time the Japanese Government has deliberately sought to deceive the United States by false statements and expressions of hope for continued peace.[23]

The USS *West Virginia* (forefront) and the USS *Tennessee* (behind) belch smoke after taking bomb and torpedo hits during the Japanese attack on Pearl Harbor. Both vessels, along with four of the six other battleships damaged in the raid, either remained in service or returned to see action in the Pacific.

Roosevelt went on to urge Congress to declare war on Japan. Less than four hours after his speech, he signed the declaration, which had passed with only one dissenting vote.

Waking a Sleeping Giant

It was Japanese admiral Isoroku Yamamoto who had planned the risky attack on Pearl Harbor and had convinced a skeptical naval general staff to approve it. The belief was that the United States, after sustaining such a sudden and staggering blow to its navy, would see that fighting a two-front war was impossible and would agree to negotiated terms, allowing Japan free rein for expansion in the Pacific. But Japan's leaders ignored a key part of Yamamoto's proposal. Yamamoto himself was quite familiar with America and the US military. He had studied at Harvard University and had served as Japan's naval attaché in Washington, DC. He had a high opinion of American character, its strength and determination, and he also knew US industrial capacity would be decisive if turned to wartime use against a hostile power like Japan. In Yamamoto's view, for the Pearl Harbor attack to succeed, it had to achieve total destruction of the American fleet. A merely crippling blow that allowed the United States to regroup and retaliate would result, however long it might take, in Japan's defeat. If Japanese leaders had any doubts that the attack would be overwhelming, they should think again about starting an all-out war with the United States.

"Yesterday, December 7, 1941—a date which will live in infamy—the United States of America was suddenly and deliberately attacked by naval and air forces of the Empire of Japan."[23]

—President Franklin D. Roosevelt, addressing Congress on the day after the Pearl Harbor attack.

Yamamoto's reservations proved correct. Vice Admiral Nagumo, a cautious commander, had decided against a third wave of strikes on Pearl Harbor's fuel depots and repair facilities, seeking to avoid a possible counterattack by US submarines. Since the US Navy's three aircraft carriers were not in port at Pearl Harbor when the Japanese attacked, a vital part of America's naval force survived to play a key role in the Pacific war. The possibility of launching a panic-inducing assault on the California coast was also rejected. Thus, the Pearl Harbor attack, while devastating, was not a knockout punch.

In *Tora! Tora! Tora!*, a 1970 Hollywood film about Pearl Harbor, the actor playing Yamamoto says, "I fear we have awakened a sleeping giant and filled him with a terrible resolve."[24] Historians now question whether the real Yamamoto ever spoke or wrote those words, but the quote expresses what seem to be the admiral's genuine doubts about the attack.

America Responds to the Attack

The Japanese attack on Pearl Harbor galvanized the United States. Anger at Japan's treachery and calls for revenge were widespread. Newspapers of all political stripes weighed in with fiery editorials in support of Roosevelt. All at once a country that had wavered and debated on the wisdom of going to war set about arming itself with a grim determination. Recruiting offices stayed open all night to handle the flood of Americans volunteering for service. Training for new pilots was curtailed at first by an insufficient number of planes. Citizens too old or too young for duty pitched in with drives to collect paper, scrap metal, rubber, grease—anything to boost the war effort. Film stars urged the purchase of war bonds, and movies with war themes dominated the cinemas. New cars and trucks disappeared as Detroit set about making military vehicles. Billboards and posters with patriotic messages sprang up everywhere. The Hit Parade introduced songs with military themes, such as "Boogie Woogie Bugle Boy."

The powerhouse of American industry quickly joined the rush to build armaments. Many company heads were Republicans who had opposed Roosevelt's domestic policies. Now, however, concerned that America lagged behind in military strength, the industrialists set aside political differences to offer their support—and received hugely lucrative government contracts in return. The American economy proved to be one of the Allies' greatest weapons. As war historian Richard Overy writes,

> The giant plans approved by Roosevelt and Congress in the first weeks of war did not just result from America's great wealth of resources, but reflected a genuine fear of military inferiority. In

four years these plans turned America from military weakling to military super-power. American industry provided almost two-thirds of all the Allied military equipment produced during the war: 297,000 aircraft, 193,000 artillery pieces, 86,000 tanks, 2 million army trucks. In four years American industrial production, already the world's largest, doubled in size. . . . In the naval war the figures were more remarkable still: 8,800 naval vessels and 87,000 landing craft in four years. For every one major naval vessel constructed in Japanese shipyards, America produced sixteen.[25]

Workers at the Boeing aircraft plant in Seattle, Washington, assemble bombers for the war effort. Isolated from the battlefields of Europe and Asia, the United States could out-produce its allies and its enemies, making its industries a powerful weapon in the Allied arsenal.

A Strategic Blunder

Pearl Harbor also changed the course of the war in Europe, where Germany's blitzkrieg tactics had produced a string of victories and a sense of invincibility. Soon after the Japanese attack, Adolf Hitler made a hasty decision that greatly aided the Allies' cause. By declaring war on the United States, despite an agreement with Japan that did not require such an action, Hitler made it easy for Roosevelt to secure the same declaration against Germany. As a result, Roosevelt

From Pearl Harbor to Midway

After the disastrous attack at Pearl Harbor, US naval forces seemed hopelessly outnumbered and outgunned by the Japanese Imperial Navy. Japanese forces swiftly went on to invade or conquer territory throughout the Pacific and Southeast Asia, including the Philippines, Thailand, Singapore, Hong Kong, Malaya, Burma, and New Guinea. Yet the attack and its aftermath actually prepared the way for one of the most remarkable victories in American naval history. Despite the destruction of many US ships and planes at Pearl Harbor, the Japanese failed to eliminate US aircraft carriers and submarines, which were at sea when the attack occurred. This oversight would prove fatal only a few months later.

The Japanese also overreacted to the Doolittle Raid on Tokyo and other cities in Japan. Admiral Isoroku Yamamoto decided to avenge the US operation by luring the US fleet into a decisive battle at Midway, the closest American base to Japan. However, Yamamoto's plans for a trap were discovered by code breakers at US Naval Intelligence. Yamamoto intended to crush the American navy by employing almost the entire Japanese fleet—six aircraft carriers, eleven battleships, thirteen cruisers, and forty-five destroyers. Instead, it was the Japanese who were taken by surprise. On June 4, 1942, after an initial Japanese strike on the Midway base, US dive-bombers descended from a cloudy sky and attacked the Japanese ships. Soon four Japanese carriers were ablaze. The decisive US victory at Midway put Japan on the defensive for the rest of the Pacific war.

was able to keep a secret promise he had made to Churchill—that upon entering the war, America would help defeat Nazi Germany first. Thus, Pearl Harbor brought America into the fight against Germany and also served to cement the close relationship between Roosevelt and Churchill that was so important to the success of the Allies. In addition, Hitler's hopes that declaring war on Japan's enemy, the United States, would lead the Japanese to return the favor and declare war on the Soviet Union proved illusory. Japan showed no desire to divide its forces and assist the Nazis' invasion in Russia.

In the end, the attack on Pearl Harbor had disastrous consequences for Japan and the Axis powers. "From the perspective of history," writes historian Alan Axelrod, "assessing the effect of the battle of Pearl Harbor is easy. A great tactical triumph for Japan, it was a monumental strategic blunder, because it provoked a great industrial power to a massive and united war effort that ensured Japan's ultimate defeat."[26]

> "From the perspective of history, assessing the effect of the battle of Pearl Harbor is easy. . . . It was a monumental strategic blunder, because it provoked a great industrial power to a massive and united war effort that ensured Japan's ultimate defeat."[26]
>
> —Historian Alan Axelrod.

How Did the German Invasion of the Soviet Union Change the Course of the War?

Focus Questions

1. Why was the announcement of the German-Soviet Non-aggression Pact in 1939 so unexpected?
2. What effect did Hitler's failure to win the Battle of Britain have on the outcome of the war against the Soviet Union?
3. Would World War II have turned out differently if Operation Barbarossa had been a rapid success? Why or why not?

Soviet leader Joseph Stalin was cynical, pragmatic, and ruthless. He was, in fact, quite paranoid in his dealings with others, whether underlings or other heads of state. In the late 1930s, in order to tighten his grip on power, he had instituted what became known as the Great Terror. This weeding out of Communist Party members accused of disloyalty frequently resulted in execution on trumped-up charges. These purges cut down tens of thousands, including nearly half of the Soviet officer corps of eighty thousand. In short, Stalin trusted almost no one. Yet in the summer of 1939, with tensions in Europe running high, Stalin accepted an overture from Adolf Hitler regarding a possible agreement between the Soviet Union and Nazi Germany. Despite their ideological differences, Stalin seemed to view Hitler as someone he could work with, a leader like himself interested in power above all. Two of history's most prolific murderers quickly reached terms on the future of Eastern Europe.

The German-Soviet Nonaggression Pact

On August 22, 1939, German foreign minister Joachim von Ribbentrop flew to Moscow to meet with Stalin and his foreign minister, Vyacheslav Molotov. Ribbentrop delivered Hitler's proposal: a pact between their two countries pledging nonaggression for one hundred years. Stalin coolly declared that ten years would be sufficient. The agreement included secret terms that set the spheres of influence for each country following Hitler's conquest of Poland. It was agreed that the Soviets would occupy Poland's eastern half as well as Latvia, Lithuania, and Estonia. Hitler believed that after his armies had achieved more difficult victories in the west, it would be easy to overrun the Soviet Union later. Therefore, he was very accommodating to Stalin. "Whatever the Soviets wanted, they could get, including a few things they did not even ask for,"[27] says military historian Gerhard L. Weinberg. In return, Hitler received vital resources for the German war effort.

The German-Soviet pact was signed the day after Ribbentrop's arrival. The announcement on August 25 sent shock waves around the world. Observers were astonished that two nations thought to be the bitterest of enemies could reach such an agreement. For Hitler, the pact represented an astounding about-face. In his book *Mein Kampf* he had poured scorn on Bolshevism (the Russian brand of communism) and what he viewed as its unacceptable roots in Jewish thought. Upon seizing power the Nazis had outlawed Communist political meetings, and Hitler's Brown Shirts had attacked German Communists in the streets. Yet in truth, Hitler's loathing of communism was no less extreme than before. He had set aside—temporarily—his opposition to Stalin and the Soviets in order to achieve one of the great coups of his career. With one stroke Hitler seemed to have ensured that Germany would not have to fight a war on two fronts—against Britain and its allies in the west and against the Soviet Union in the east. A similar situation had proven disastrous in the last war. He also gained breathing space to consider his next moves. Subsequently, on September 1, 1939, German troops invaded Poland.

In a secret speech to the Politburo (Soviet policy makers) in Moscow on August 19, 1939, Stalin announced his own true intentions regarding the pact: "It must be our objective that Germany wage war

Prior to the invasion of Poland in September 1939, Adolf Hitler and Joseph Stalin agreed to a nonaggression pact that would allow each to seize part of Polish territory once German armies began hostilities. Here, a British newspaper seller displays headlines that reveal the shocking collaboration.

long enough to exhaust England and France so much that they cannot defeat Germany alone.... It's paramount for us that this war [between Germany and the Allies] continues as long as possible, until both sides are worn out."[28] Stalin thought that after such an exhausting conflict, the Soviet Union would be in a dominant position regarding the weakened Germans and Allies. With fresh Soviet troops at his disposal, he could dictate terms to Hitler and Allied leaders about the future of Europe.

The German Failure in the Battle of Britain

With the Soviet Union neutralized by treaty and the United States still on the sidelines, Hitler was able to pursue his conquest of Europe with little resistance. German blitzkrieg tactics toppled nations like dominoes: Poland, Belgium, the Netherlands, and northern France. These successes made Hitler, once an undistinguished corporal, believe in his own military genius. But having pushed British forces in France to the brink of the English Channel, Hitler hesitated to strike the fatal blow. The British were able to evacuate their forces at Dunkirk, moving them back across the channel against all odds. In the summer of 1940 Hitler launched an air war in the skies over Great Britain, planning to overpower the British Royal Air Force (RAF) as a prelude to a full-scale invasion. Instead, the British held out against repeated bombing raids by the Luftwaffe, the German air force. The RAF lost 915 fighter planes but shot down more than twice that number of enemy planes. Hitler feared losing too much of his airpower, and his focus had already shifted to planning an attack on what he considered Nazi Germany's main enemy, the Soviet Union. The nonaggression pact with Stalin was merely a ploy to buy time, and Hitler's hatred of communism certainly drove his war strategy. Nonetheless, Hitler's willingness to abandon the British campaign in favor of a concentrated attack on Communist Russia continues to puzzle historians of the war.

Although the Luftwaffe continued bombing raids on London and other British cities for several months, Germany had essentially lost the Battle of Britain by November 1940. Operation Sea Lion, the German plan for the invasion of Britain, was called off. In tribute to the stalwart British pilots, Prime Minister Winston Churchill said, "Never in the field of human conflict was so much owed by so many to so few."[29]

The Nazi Invasion of the Soviet Union

Despite having failed to obtain Britain's surrender, Hitler went ahead with plans to invade the Soviet Union. It proved to be a reckless decision. "Hitler needed someone—anyone—in his close circle to remind him of the perils of invading Russia," notes historian Andrew Roberts. Foremost among these perils were the sheer size of the country and the dreaded Russian winter with its treacherous mud, snow, and ice. "Yet he believed, as he told [Field Marshal Gerd von] Rundstedt, 'You have only to kick in the door, and the whole rotten structure will come crashing down.'"[30] Hitler was certain the Soviet military was weak since Stalin had purged his most experienced officers and the Red Army had only recently struggled to overcome the armies of Finland. As he wrote in *Mein Kampf*, Hitler saw the conquest of Russia as his destiny. The triumph would provide living space for the Aryan German race, bring about a reckoning for millions of Jews, and convince Britain that further resistance was futile. Even if his closest advisers had warned against the invasion, it is unlikely that Hitler would have listened. The very scale of the enterprise—code-named Operation Barbarossa—seemed to excite him. "When Barbarossa begins," he told one of his field marshals, "the world will hold its breath."[31]

> "When [Operation] Barbarossa begins, the world will hold its breath."[31]
>
> —German chancellor Adolf Hitler.

Historians have pointed out opportunities Hitler missed at this point of the war. Before attacking the Soviet Union, he could have first seized British possessions in Egypt and the Middle East. This would have deprived Allied forces of desperately needed oil in any attempt to gain a foothold in Europe. Also, Hitler did not try to enlist Japan's aid in the coming action against the Soviets. Had Japanese forces also attacked in Russia, perhaps from the Siberian north, Stalin would have faced the sort of two-front war that Hitler feared. Hitler's single-minded aim of defeating the Soviet Union in a glorious headlong campaign contributed to Germany's downfall.

The actual campaign began around 3:00 a.m. on June 22, 1941. German aircraft, tanks, and troops swept into Soviet Russia in a three-pronged attack across a 930-mile (1,497 km) front extending from Finland to Romania. Operation Barbarossa was the largest invasion in history. The blitzkrieg attack included a combined force of 3.6 million German and Axis soldiers and thirty-six hundred tanks. The Soviets knew in advance of large German troop movements on their border but were not prepared for how quickly these troops could be deployed as a strike force. Reports on the day before the invasion of German planes flying reconnaissance missions over Russian territory barely stirred the Soviet high command. Warnings to Red Army units were tentative and late. Some historians speculate that the Soviet chief of military intelligence may have been reluctant to deliver the disastrous news to the unpredictable Stalin. Upon learning the truth, Stalin, the fabled man of steel, nearly had a breakdown. The general who telephoned at 3:30 a.m. to inform the Soviet leader about the attack had to repeat himself, hearing only heavy breathing on the line. An hour later a white-faced Stalin was obviously still in shock when he met

A German armored vehicle steers past wreckage in the later stages of Operation Barbarossa. The invasion of the Soviet Union was swift and successful through the first year of fighting, but Soviet manpower, the nation's vastness, and the harshness of Russian winters eventually slowed the advances.

Historians have often asked why Hitler turned so quickly from the Battle of Britain to invade the Soviet Union. Had he concentrated first on defeating the British, the German conquest of Russia might well have become impossible to stop. However, from the start of his political career, Hitler was a person in a hurry. He felt it was his destiny to deliver lebensraum, or living space, for future generations of Germans. He considered himself indispensable to Germany's drive to dominate the world. On one hand, this belief in destiny led him to overestimate his skill as a military planner. On the other, it made him rush to accomplish all he could before his fragile health gave out.

As a corporal on the western front during World War I, Hitler had suffered a poison-gas attack. Temporarily blinded, he also contracted meningitis and Parkinson's disease, the latter a nerve disorder that left him with a permanent tremble in his left hand. The episode brought on persistent worries that his life would be short. As führer (leader), he obsessed about his health. As he told his staff in 1941, "With age, optimism gets weaker. The spring relaxes. When I suffered my setback in 1923 [imprisoned after a failed coup attempt], I had only one idea, to get back into the saddle. Today I'd no longer be capable of the effort which that implies." Hitler's concern about his own longevity probably helped bring about Germany's crushing defeat at the hands of the Soviets.

Quoted in H.R. Trevor-Roper, ed., *Hitler's Table Talk, 1941–1944: His Private Conversations.* New York: Enigma, 2008, p. 132.

with the Politburo. His first orders to Red Army commanders were vague and contradictory. For a week after the invasion, Stalin retired to his dacha (country house) outside Moscow while the machinery of the Soviet government almost ground to a halt awaiting his commands.

Early Success and a Costly Mistake

At first the Germans rampaged through Soviet defenses almost unopposed. Soviet superiority in numbers of men and machinery made little difference. Red Army troops were poorly trained and haphazardly deployed due to Stalin's purges of experienced officers. Soviet aircraft and tanks were woefully out of date and no match for their Nazi counterparts. Within hours of the invasion, Nazi bombers had laid waste to more than sixty Soviet airfields, leaving scores of destroyed planes in their wake. In the first week of combat 90 percent of the Red Army's tank corps was demolished. In less than a month the Germans, arrayed in three massive army groups, had covered 400 miles (645 km), overwhelmed millions of Soviet troops, severed supply lines, and cut off reinforcements. The Red Army verged on total collapse. As German forces plunged deep into Soviet territory, it looked as if Hitler's gamble would pay off in a swift, decisive victory.

Two factors combined to stop the Nazis' momentum. The first was Stalin's ability to recover from his dazed initial reaction and rally the Russian people to defend their homeland. A further 5 million personnel, including hundreds of thousands of women, were mobilized to fight the German invaders. Volunteers dug antitank ditches and set up machine-gun nests. Those who lacked guns or grenades made so-called Molotov cocktails—gasoline-filled bottles stuffed with rags that could be set alight and thrown at the enemy. Stalin called on Soviet citizens to make a grand sacrifice for the cause. In a nationwide radio broadcast on July 3, 1941, he referred to the struggle as the Great Patriotic War, and he even revived the Russian Orthodox Church despite the Communists' hatred of religion. It was probably the first time the Soviet government won the people's full support.

The second factor was Hitler's weakness as a strategist. With victory over the Soviet Union in his grasp, he once more made a fatal error. His generals knew the key ingredient to success in Operation Barbarossa was speed. The Soviets had to be defeated quickly with blitzkrieg tactics. Should the fighting extend into the Russian winter, with its subzero temperatures and relentless ice and snow, the consequences would likely be disastrous for Germany. When German forces easily broke through the Soviet forward defenses and then captured Smolensk 220 miles (354 km) southwest of Moscow, the Nazis' victory seemed assured. Yet instead of instantly continuing on to Moscow, the Soviet capital and nerve center, as his general staff urged, Hitler ordered one of his most effective armies diverted to Ukraine in the south. Although the maneuver was a tactical success, leading to the capture of six hundred thousand prisoners and the acquisition of oil and other resources, the delay proved disastrous for the Germans. As Jim Lacey, a professor at the Marine Corps War College, observes,

When the advance on Moscow—Operation Typhoon—was renewed on October 2, a precious month had been lost. A combination of stubborn Russian resistance, German overextension, and abysmal weather soon stalled the German offensive just short of its ultimate objective. . . . Hitler's chance for a quick and decisive outcome in the East dissolved.[32]

Soviet Victories at Moscow and Stalingrad

By December, with Moscow almost in sight, the German army had ground to a halt, its tanks and other machinery stymied first by mud and then by freezing temperatures and heavy snow. "Vehicles no longer started, engines froze while they ran, breaches of artillery pieces froze shut, tank turrets froze solid and machine guns jammed,"[33] says American historian Craig Luther. German soldiers were not equipped for winter combat, so confident had Hitler's general staff been of the Red Army's rapid collapse. In addition, Hitler and his officers had not counted on the stubborn determination of Russian soldiers and citizens, their ability to absorb losses and keep fighting. Having traveled hundreds of miles across the Russian frontier, German forces were exhausted and freezing and their supply lines were stretched to the breaking point. In fighting that spared nothing and no one, the Germans had destroyed Soviet crops, barns, and warehouses along the way. Now, on Stalin's orders, the Red Army burned their own fields and villages so that the Germans could not make use of them. Hitler's stubborn refusal to allow his armies to

> "A combination of stubborn Russian resistance, German overextension, and abysmal weather soon stalled the German offensive just short of its ultimate objective. ... Hitler's chance for a quick and decisive outcome in the East dissolved."[32]
>
> —Jim Lacey, professor at the Marine Corps War College.

retreat and regroup for a spring offensive left German soldiers haggard and sluggish. The ability of the Red Army to dig in and then launch a series of counterattacks, however costly, turned the tide in the battle for Moscow. With the failure of Operation Barbarossa, the idea of Hitler as an invincible conqueror fell apart.

One month into 1942, losses on both sides were staggering. Approximately 910,000 German soldiers—nearly 30 percent of the invasion force—had been killed, wounded, or captured. Casualties for the Red Army numbered about 3.3 million, yet the large population

With German armies poised outside Moscow in December 1941, the fierce Soviet winter hit. The German army expected a quicker victory and had not equipped its men or vehicles to face the cold. Numerous troops suffered debilitating frostbite, and tanks and trucks froze up in the low temperatures.

in Russia enabled the Soviets to sustain such lopsided losses. After Moscow the main fighting shifted to the Battle of Stalingrad, which lasted from July 17, 1942, to February 2, 1943. Stalingrad, an industrial city on the Volga River in southern Russia, was prized by Hitler as much for the symbolism of its name as its importance to the Soviet war effort. On September 30, 1942, Hitler boasted in a public speech, "The occupation of Stalingrad, which will also be carried through, will deepen this gigantic victory and strengthen it, and you can be sure that

The Commissar Order

The war between Hitler's invasion force and the Soviet Union was one of the cruelest, bloodiest conflicts in history. From the beginning no mercy was shown on either side. For Hitler, the goal was not simply victory on the battlefield but rather total annihilation of the Russian Communists.

On June 6, 1941, about two weeks before the invasion, the German high command issued the notorious Commissar Order. It was a license for Nazi commanders to ignore international rules of war and commit atrocities against the Soviet Union. The written order—seen at once to be explosive—was delivered to only the most senior Nazi military officers. They were instructed to inform the lower ranks verbally. Commissars were political agents whose job was to ensure the Communist Party maintained control over every aspect of the Soviet military. Hitler regarded them as carriers of the political disease that had to be eliminated. According to the order, "These commissars are not to be recognized as soldiers; the protection due to prisoners of war under international law does not apply to them. When they have been separated, they are to be finished off."

The Commissar Order doubtless served to stiffen the will of both Russian soldiers and citizens. They quickly realized that the invading Nazis aimed to wipe out the Soviet Union entirely. In May 1942, after German field commanders complained that its main effect was to increase resistance among the Soviets, the order was canceled.

Quoted in World War II Today, "Hitler Orders All Soviet Commissars to Be Shot." http://ww2today.com.

no human being will drive us out of this place later on."[34] The German army's months-long siege of the city led finally to brutal hand-to-hand fighting in streets and alleyways. Neither Hitler nor Stalin would allow his forces to take a step back, as troops on both sides were continually fed into the meat grinder of close combat. At the end, German soldiers—tired, starving, and low on ammunition—were reduced to fighting in the sewers. Only 91,000 remained alive when German field marshal Friedrich Paulus surrendered at last.

A Fatal Conceit

Germany's failure to achieve a rapid victory over the Soviets enabled Stalin's Red Army to regroup and eventually repel the invading Nazi armies. After Stalingrad, German forces began a retreat westward with the Red Army in hot pursuit. With the United States joining the Allied effort in western Europe, Hitler's strategic blunders landed him in the two-front war he had been warned to avoid. Morale in Germany continued to collapse with each disastrous report from the battlefield, as German troops were squeezed by the Allies advancing in the west and the Soviets in the east. "Anyone can do the little job of directing operations in war,"[35] Hitler had announced to his general staff. It was a fatal conceit that led to the Nazis' downfall in World War II.

> "Anyone can do the little job of directing operations in war."[35]
>
> —Nazi leader Adolf Hitler.

How Did the End of World War II Contribute to the Start of the Cold War?

Focus Questions

1. Was Stalin justified in seeking a buffer zone in Eastern Europe to protect the Soviet Union from attack? Why or why not?
2. Was the United States or the Soviet Union chiefly responsible for the Cold War? Explain your answer.
3. Why do you think the policy of containment, as employed by the United States, was so successful?

The alliance between the United States and the Soviet Union began to fall apart even before World War II was over. Both sides could foresee competition ahead for influence in Europe and other areas of the world. "While liberating Eastern Europe from Nazi Germany in World War II," writes Library of Congress scholar Glenn E. Curtis, "the Red Army established political and military control over that region. The Soviet Union's size, economic weight, and sheer military power made its domination inevitable in this part of Europe."[36] Beginning in 1943 Stalin's generals had organized units made up of Polish, Czechoslovakian, and other refugee soldiers in Soviet territory. The units would join Soviet forces on their westward offensive against the Nazis. Soviet political officers instilled these foreign troops with Communist ideology, laying the groundwork for their loyalty after the war. As the Red Army pursued German troops back across Eastern Europe, Stalin seemed satisfied that his forces not proceed too rapidly. A slower advance resulted in more devastation in Eastern European countries already rocked by war. Nations in a ruined state, Stalin believed, would be ripe for Communist takeover. Instead of being liberated by Soviet troops, Eastern Europe would trade one occupying force for another.

The Yalta Conference

The basis for Soviet domination of Eastern Europe was set during eight days at Yalta, a Russian resort town located on the Black Sea. In February 1945, with the Allied victory in sight, the so-called Big Three leaders—Roosevelt, Churchill, and Stalin—met at Yalta to plan the fate of postwar Europe. Roosevelt saw Stalin as someone with whom he could do business. After their first meeting Roosevelt had said, "We got on beautifully. We cracked the ice, if there ever was any ice; and since then there has been no ice."[37] Churchill was more wary of the Soviet leader. Stalin insisted that the conference be held in Soviet territory, requiring his fellow Allied leaders to travel long distances. Some observers perceived this as a not-so-subtle sign that Stalin intended to dominate the conference. The American and British delegations were housed in luxurious accommodations, with all the rooms bugged by the Soviet secret police.

> "We got on beautifully. We cracked the ice, if there ever was any ice; and since then there has been no ice."[37]
>
> —President Franklin D. Roosevelt.

Each leader had a specific agenda. Churchill wanted to preserve, as much as possible, Britain's empire. Roosevelt sought Stalin's promise to enter the Pacific war and a general agreement to participate in the United Nations. However, Stalin's goals were more specific: the expansion of Soviet-controlled territory. Regarding the future of Poland, Stalin said, "For the Russian people, the question of Poland is not only a question of honor but also a question of security. Throughout history, Poland has been the corridor through which the enemy has passed into Russia. Poland is a question of life and death for Russia."[38] Thus, Stalin demanded that Poland, like other Eastern European nations, form a buffer zone protecting the USSR from attack.

In the end, the Big Three agreed to terms that outlined the postwar world. Roosevelt was delighted to get Stalin's assurances to help fight

In 1945, (L to R) Winston Churchill, Franklin Roosevelt, and Joseph Stalin met at a Russian resort town primarily to discuss the shape of the postwar world. Among other things, the three agreed to the splitting of Germany into occupation zones and the reestablishment of most prewar national governments.

Japan, although the Soviet leader's support would be delayed until several weeks after Germany's surrender. Agreement also was reached on the United Nations. Its main body, the Security Council, would consist of five permanent members—the United States, the Soviet Union, Great Britain, France, and China—and six rotating, nonpermanent members (later expanded to ten). The five permanent members would each have veto power in Security Council actions.

The three leaders also agreed to grant France one of the four occupation zones in Germany and Austria. The question of Poland, however, brought less satisfactory results for Roosevelt and Churchill. Stalin insisted it become part of the Soviet sphere. His promise of free elections in Poland rang hollow since the Red Army already occupied Polish territory. "The Western delegates at Yalta had little choice but to accept the fact of preponderant [dominant] Soviet power," writes historian S.M. Plokhy. "Roosevelt believed that subjecting Stalin to greater pressure would bring no results. Churchill disagreed and wanted further discussions, but there is no indication whatever that Stalin was prepared to compromise on Poland. The country was too important in his scheme of things to loosen his grip on it."[39]

Roosevelt returned home with optimistic words about future US-Soviet cooperation. Yet privately Roosevelt also had doubts. As Plokhy relates,

> When Admiral [William D.] Leahy, who was not involved in the actual negotiations on the [Polish] issue, told Roosevelt, "Mr. President, this [agreement] is so elastic that the Russians can stretch it all the way from Yalta to Washington, without ever technically breaking it," he was told, "I know, Bill, I know it. But it's the best I can do for Poland at this time."[40]

Tensions Increase Between the Superpowers

On April 12, 1945, President Roosevelt died suddenly of a massive stroke. Roosevelt's failing health had been apparent for months, leading some to blame his lack of strength for what they saw as his disastrous capitulation to Stalin at Yalta. Roosevelt's successor, Harry S. Truman, oversaw the end of the war in Germany and Japan. Upon taking office, Truman knew nothing about the atomic bomb and its potential for mass destruction. A few months later he made the decision to use the weapon twice, at Hiroshima and Nagasaki, to force the surrender of the Japanese. America's deployment of the atomic bomb left no doubt that a new world order was at hand. The United States, which so recently had balked at playing a large role in global affairs, had replaced Great Britain as the world's dominant power. Its military and economic strength was unchallenged. "We have emerged from this war the most powerful nation in the world," Truman declared, "the most powerful nation, perhaps, in all history."[41]

For all its losses in the war, the Soviet Union also emerged as a powerful force in Eastern Europe and Asia. Victory over Nazi Germany had given the Communist Party in Russia new confidence. The USSR, with its own proven military and industrial prowess, touted its system of government as the world's future—the best alternative to capitalism and imperialism. Soviet assertiveness arose in its policy toward refugees in Europe. Stalin did little to cooperate with the newly chartered United Nations and its relief group, the United Nations Relief and Rehabilitation Administration (UNRRA).

> "We have emerged from this war the most powerful nation in the world, the most powerful nation, perhaps, in all history."[41]
>
> —President Harry S. Truman on the US position in the postwar world.

The Red Army refused to hand over to the UNRRA displaced persons (DPs) in Soviet-controlled territory, including Jews who had survived the Nazi death camps. Instead, these refugees received the bare minimum of care and often were sent to forced labor camps. Once they learned about conditions on the Soviet side, many DPs risked their lives to reach US-controlled DP facilities in Western Europe. The Soviets also took advantage of the partitioning of Germany and Austria into zones of influence. The zones were set up as temporary boundaries to help the Allies administer enemy territory, including badly depleted cities and towns. Stalin, however, used the Russian zone to tighten his grip on eastern Germany and gain a foothold in Europe. Eventually the USSR would exert control over Communist governments in so-called satellite states across Eastern Europe.

Immediately after the war, American leaders believed peaceful relations with their recent ally were still possible. "I don't believe the Reds want a war," General Dwight D. Eisenhower told President Truman and his Joint Chiefs of Staff in June 1946. "What can they gain now by armed conflict? They've gained just about all they can assimilate."[42] Nevertheless, tensions in Europe brought about a chill between the United States and the Soviet Union. With the Nazis defeated, most Americans returned to their prewar anti-Communist sentiments. Newspapers and magazines warned about Communist expansion in Europe and Asia. Stalin, often referred to as "Uncle Joe" during the war, was increasingly viewed as a scheming tyrant. After Hitler's example of broken promises and wars of conquest, many in the West feared one of two outcomes was inevitable: either the West would appease Stalin's thirst for expansion or there would be war with the Soviet Union.

The Potsdam Conference

The Yalta Conference is famous for being President Franklin D. Roosevelt's final appearance on the world stage and for Joseph Stalin's insistence on control of Eastern Europe. Yet the Allies' final conference at Potsdam, Germany, held a few months later in July 1945, also helped shape the postwar world. Meeting at Potsdam were President Harry S. Truman, Prime Minister Winston Churchill, and Soviet leader Stalin. Churchill, after losing the general election in Britain, was replaced at Potsdam on July 26 by the new prime minister, Clement Attlee. Some issues at the conference met with broad agreement, such as setting the terms of Japan's surrender and deciding to hold Nazi war-crimes trials. Other questions about Germany proved harder to settle.

Relations between Stalin and his fellow Allied leaders had soured a great deal since Yalta. In March 1945 Stalin had staged a meeting with non-Communist Polish leaders only to have them arrested. British planners had outlined their response, known as Operation Unthinkable, in case of war with Russia. And, unlike his predecessor, Truman favored a tougher approach with Stalin. A major sticking point at Potsdam was the issue of how much Germany should pay in war reparations. Stalin insisted on large payments to punish the Germans—a demand that reminded some of the Treaty of Versailles of 1919, which bankrupted Germany and eventually inspired Hitler's revenge. In the end, the Soviets were allowed to seize larger reparations in their zone of control. But an underlying bitterness at Potsdam would mark Cold War relations going forward.

The Policy of Containment

One person who saw a third possibility for US-Soviet relations was George F. Kennan, a career US diplomat based in Moscow. Kennan, a student of Russian literature and history, had helped set up the first American embassy in the Soviet Union in 1933. Over the years, as an eyewitness to forced collectivization and political terror in Russia, he became much more pessimistic regarding Stalin and the Politburo. He believed President Roosevelt was misguided in his attempts to develop a friendly relationship with the cunning Stalin. In February 1946, several months after Roosevelt's death, Kennan put his thoughts about Stalin and the Soviet Union into the so-called Long Telegram, probably the most influential foreign policy document of the post-war years. He followed this with an anonymous article in a magazine called *Foreign Affairs.* In these writings, Kennan outlined a policy toward the Soviet Union that he termed *containment.* It lay between the extremes of appeasing the Russians—allowing them to expand without opposition—and fighting a deadly war. The idea was to contain, or limit, Soviet aggression in the world. As John Lewis Gaddis, Kennan's biographer, explains,

> Stalin, [Kennan] said, is not Hitler. He does not have a fixed timetable for aggression. He is determined to dominate Europe and, if possible, the world, but there is no hurry about it. If the US and its allies could be patient and contain Soviet expansionism without war or appeasement over a sufficiently long period of time the Russians would change their priorities. . . . Kennan foresaw internal contradictions within the Soviet system that would probably cause it to fall apart.[43]

Kennan's ideas drew plenty of criticism. Some political writers in the United States and elsewhere in the West called for a more aggressive response to the Soviet Union and its Communist allies. Nevertheless, Truman agreed with the basic approach, and containment became US policy. As opposed to an all-out hot war on the battlefield, the strategy was dubbed the *Cold War* by presidential adviser Bernard Baruch.

The Berlin Blockade and Airlift

Initially Cold War tensions between the United States and the Soviet Union edged closer to open hostility. Truman worried about the spread of communism in Eastern Europe. In March 1947 he responded to Communist revolts in Greece and Turkey by announcing the Truman Doctrine. This was a promise to support and defend free people who were trying to resist takeover by armed minorities—in other words, a pledge to stop Communist subversion. Three months later the United States launched the Marshall Plan, named for Secretary of State George C. Marshall. This was a program that bolstered the Truman Doctrine by providing money and supplies to rebuild Europe. By promoting swift economic recovery, the United States and its allies hoped to head off the advance of communism in nations still struggling amid the wreckage of war. Funding for the Marshall Plan eventually totaled $12 billion. European industry surged back to life, investment in Europe increased, and American companies benefited from expanded markets.

Stalin and the Soviets saw the Marshall Plan as an American attempt to dominate Europe, particularly Germany. American aid was restricted to Western European nations, and even had it been offered to the East, Stalin would have refused opening those tightly controlled societies to capitalist dollars. At any rate, the impression grew that Soviet bloc nations were falling behind the West.

> "If the US and its allies could be patient and contain Soviet expansionism without war or appeasement over a sufficiently long period of time the Russians would change their priorities. . . . Kennan foresaw internal contradictions within the Soviet system that would probably cause it to fall apart."[43]
>
> —John Lewis Gaddis, George F. Kennan's biographer.

By June 1948 the Western powers, including the United States, Great Britain, and France, had concluded they could no longer work with the Soviet Union on plans to rebuild a partitioned Germany. Stalin rejected the idea of unifying the Western and Eastern (or Soviet-controlled) sectors of Germany. A particular sticking point was the city of Berlin, located in the middle of the Soviet sector. Like postwar Germany itself, Berlin was divided into four parts, with the Soviet part representing half the city. In London, the Western powers agreed to join their sectors into a West German state with its own government and a new currency, the deutsche mark. This decision enraged Stalin, leading to the first overt aggressive act of the Cold War. On June 24, 1948, the day after the new currency was introduced, the Soviets imposed a total blockade on Berlin. No rail or truck shipments

West Berliners welcome a cargo plane carrying supplies to their half of the Soviet-blockaded city. Although Stalin hoped Berlin would fall peacefully to his blockade, the aircraft of the Western Allies kept West Berliners supplied for a year until the Soviets permitted rail and road access to resume.

from the Western zones were allowed into the city. Soon, canal traffic was also halted. Since the Soviets had set no terms with the Western powers about ground access to Berlin, Stalin could claim there was no breach of international law. He was gambling that the West would back down, allowing the Soviets to take control of all of Berlin.

Instead, the United States and the Western allies organized the Berlin Airlift. This was a massive effort to thwart the blockade by flying food and supplies to the people of West Berlin. The airlift continued for nearly a year, included more than 277,000 flights, and was able to deliver about 13,000 tons (11,793 metric t) of supplies each day. There was some irony in the fact of former Allied pilots now risking their lives for Berliners. As American historian Richard Reeves notes, "This time they were supposed to feed the people they had been trying to kill, and who had been trying to kill them, only three years earlier."[44] In May 1949 Stalin finally lifted the blockade, but the battle lines of the Cold War had been drawn.

> "This time they were supposed to feed the people they had been trying to kill, and who had been trying to kill them, only three years earlier."[44]
>
> —American historian Richard Reeves.

NATO and the Korean War

Soviet aggression in the Berlin Blockade led the United States and other Western nations to consider a new alliance in Europe. Truman feared that Stalin might try to intimidate countries in Western Europe into making hasty deals to avoid war. The American president wanted an agreement that would commit the United States to the security of Western Europe. Such a pact would follow UN guidelines but still avoid the Security Council, where the Soviets could veto any American action. Despite general agreement among the Western nations, working out the details of a collective security treaty took several months. For example, Western Europe's leaders sought assurance that the United States would automatically come to their defense in case of attack. Yet according to the US Constitution, only Congress can declare war. Western European countries also needed massive American aid to rebuild their defenses. To demonstrate its commitment to Europe's security, the Truman administration set up a peacetime draft and increased military spending. Finally, in 1949, twelve nations signed an agreement that created the North Atlantic Treaty Organization (NATO). Among the twelve original members were the United States, Great Britain, France, and Canada. Shortly afterward, Truman pushed the Mutual Defense Assistance Program through Congress, obtaining $1.4 billion in military aid for Western Europe. For the first time in its history, the United States had joined a peacetime military alliance outside the Western Hemisphere. NATO was further proof that the United States was now a global power.

That same year, however, it became apparent that the United States was not the world's only military superpower. In August the Soviet Union successfully exploded its first atomic bomb. American officials were shocked that the Soviets were able to develop nuclear capability so quickly. This was another major reason for the United States to ramp up its weaponry, both conventional and nuclear. Soon, Truman's willingness to oppose the spread of Soviet influence was put to the test. In June 1950 armies of North Korea invaded South Korea, seeking to unify the country under Communist rule. Whereas the Soviet Union and China backed North Korean forces, the United States, with support from the United Nations, formed an alliance to defend South Korea. After three years and the loss of more than 2 million lives, the conflict ended with an uneasy truce that continues to this day.

The Legacy of the Cold War

The Korean War set a pattern for Cold War competition between the United States and the Soviet Union and their allies. Time and again, from Africa to Southeast Asia to Latin America, the Soviets offered support for revolutionary movements that the United States opposed as fronts for Communist tyranny. Despite years of antagonism, the two dominant powers avoided a shooting war with each other, and nuclear missiles on both sides never left their silos. In the 1980s a massive military buildup in America left the Soviet Union unable to compete and revealed the Soviet economy to be much weaker than many Western analysts had assumed. In 1989 the Soviet-built Berlin Wall came down to much fanfare. For the first time since World War

The Cultural Cold War

The Cold War between the Western democracies and the Soviet Union played out in many venues, from third-world revolutions to book review pages in the Western press. One area of lively competition between the two sides was culture, particularly music and literature. After the war Stalin immediately saw how culture could be employed as propaganda for the Soviet system. "Experts in the use of culture as a tool of political persuasion," writes historian Frances Stonor Saunders, "the Soviets did much in these early years of the Cold War to establish its central paradigm as a cultural one. Lacking the economic power of the United States . . . Stalin's regime concentrated on winning 'the battle for men's minds.'" Russian orchestras and opera companies staged performances for European audiences starved for great music. The intended message was that Soviet culture was superior to that of the West, and especially the gum-chewing, wisecracking Americans.

In response, Western intellectuals organized the Congress for Cultural Freedom. The congress sponsored its own music festivals in Europe, with brilliant American orchestras, singers, and dancers performing dozens of classics. Writers such as William Faulkner and Katherine Anne Porter were enlisted to give lectures, and *Encounter,* a British literary magazine backed by the congress, drew widespread praise. Years later, however, it was revealed that the CIA had secretly funded the Congress for Cultural Freedom. This led some to label it a propaganda tool, one just as devious as those the Soviets had used.

Frances Stonor Saunders, "The Cultural Cold War: The CIA and the World of Arts and Letters," *New York Times.* www.nytimes.com.

II, Berlin became a unified city. The breakup of the Soviet Union in December 1991 seemed to fulfill Kennan's postwar blueprint for winning the Cold War. The fight against totalitarian societies that began in World War II had reached a peaceful end.

One surprising legacy of the Cold War was the economic success of the former Axis powers. Germany and Japan rejected the militarism

The tearing down of the Berlin Wall in 1989 symbolized the crumbling of Soviet power in Europe. The subsequent collapse of the Soviet Union in 1991 signaled to many the end of the Cold War and the long hoped-for commitment to democracy in former Eastern Bloc countries.

in their recent past as well as the lure of communism, and they remade themselves into economic powerhouses firmly allied to the United States and the West. Japanese foreign minister Saburo Okita recalled how, after Japan's defeat, its people nursed hopes for the future: "It's miserable now, but in time Japan will get back on its feet again, not through military power, but by new technology and economic power."[45] Overall, the West's pursuit of the Cold War, despite its occasional over-reach and paranoia, helped produce a postwar world that was largely stable and prosperous.

Introduction: Memories of Pearl Harbor

1. Quoted in Peter Holley, "With Their Numbers Shrinking, Pearl Harbor Survivors Make Final Pilgrimages to Hawaii," *Washington Post*, December 7, 2014. www.washingtonpost.com.
2. Quoted in *Sources of British History*, "Neville Chamberlain: 'Peace for Our Time,' September 30, 1938." www.britannia.com.
3. Joel B. Pollak, "Obama: Peace in Our Time," Breitbart News Network, January 22, 2013. www.breitbart.com.

Chapter One: The Allies Defeat the Axis Powers

4. Quoted in World War II, "Fascist Italy." http://worldwar2history site.weebly.com.
5. Quoted in Richard Langworth, *Churchill by Himself: The Definitive Collection of Quotations*. New York: Public Affairs, 2011, p. 257.
6. Richard Overy, "The Battle of Britain: The Many and the Few," *History Today*, September 9, 2010. www.historytoday.com.
7. Churchill Society London, "The End of the Beginning." www .churchill-society-london.org.uk.
8. History Place, "Catastrophe at Stalingrad." www.historyplace.com.
9. Quoted in Daily Beast, "D-Day Historian Craig Symonds Talks About History's Most Amazing Invasion," June 5, 2014. www.the dailybeast.com.
10. Kenneth T. Jackson, "World War II," Gilder Lehrman Institute of American History. www.gilderlehrman.org.

Chapter Two: How Did the Treaty of Versailles Contribute to Hitler's Rise?

11. Avalon Project: Documents in Law, History, and Diplomacy, "President Woodrow Wilson's Fourteen Points." http://avalon.law .yale.edu.
12. Stephen Clarke, *1000 Years of Annoying the French*. New York: Open Road Integrated Media, 2012.

13. Quoted in History Learning Site, "The German Reaction to the Treaty of Versailles." www.historylearningsite.co.uk.

14. Quoted in Philip Scranton, "Why John Maynard Keynes Supported the New Deal," Bloomberg View, July 8, 2013. www.bloombergview.com.

15. Quoted in Michael Seear, *An Introduction to International Health.* Toronto: Canadian Scholars', 2007, p. 63.

16. Quoted in George Henry Seldes, *Facts and Fascism.* New York: In Fact, 1943, p. 157.

17. Wolfgang Mommsen, "Versailles Treaty—from the German POV," PBS. www.pbs.org.

Chapter Three: How Did the Japanese Attack on Pearl Harbor Influence the War's Outcome?

18. Quoted in Doris Kearnes Goodwin, *No Ordinary Time: Franklin & Eleanor Roosevelt: The Home Front in World War II.* New York: Simon & Schuster, 1994, p. 265.

19. Susan Townsend, "Japan's Quest for Empire, 1931–1945," BBC, March 30, 2011. www.bbc.co.uk.

20. Quoted in Joseph E. Persico, *Roosevelt's Secret War: FDR and World War II Espionage.* New York: Random House, 2002, p. 123.

21. Steven M. Gillon, *Pearl Harbor: FDR Leads the Nation into War.* New York: Basic, 2011, p. 22.

22. Quoted in Avalon Project: Documents in Law, History, and Diplomacy, "Japanese Note to the United States, December 7, 1941," http://avalon.law.yale.edu.

23. Franklin Delano Roosevelt, "Pearl Harbor Address to the Nation," American Rhetoric: Top 100 Speeches. www.americanrhetoric.com.

24. Quoted in Crosby Day, "Yamamoto's 'Sleeping Giant' Quote Awakens a Gigantic Argument," *Sun Sentinel* (South Florida), October 28, 2001. http://articles.sun-sentinel.com.

25. Richard Overy, *Why the Allies Won.* New York: W.W. Norton, 1995, pp. 191–92.

26. Alan Axelrod, *The Real History of World War II: A New Look at the Past.* New York: Sterling, 2008, p. 152.

Chapter Four: How Did the German Invasion of the Soviet Union Change the Course of the War?

27. Gerhard L. Weinberg, "The Nazi-Soviet Pacts: A Half-Century Later," *Foreign Affairs*, Fall 1989. www.foreignaffairs.com.

28. Quoted in Richard Tedor, "Stalin's Secret War Plans: Why Hitler Invaded the Soviet Union," Scriptorium, 2002. www.wintersonnenwende.com.

29. Winston Churchill, "Premier's Review of the War," *Guardian* (Manchester, UK), August 21, 1940. www.theguardian.com.

30. Andrew Roberts, *The Storm of War: A New History of the Second World War*. New York: HarperCollins, 2011, p. 143.

31. Quoted in David Stahel, *Operation Barbarossa and Germany's Defeat in the East*. New York: Cambridge University Press, 2009, p. 1.

32. Jim Lacey, "Hitler's Greatest Blunders," History Net. www.historynet.com.

33. Quoted in Vincent Vicini, "Military History Lecture Features Hitler's Russian Mistake," *Spartan Daily* (San Jose State University), October 12, 2014. http://spartandaily.com.

34. Adolf Hitler, "Address at the Opening of the Winter Relief Campaign," Jewish Virtual Library. www.jewishvirtuallibrary.org.

35. Quoted in Tony Le Tissier, *Zhukov at the Oder: The Decisive Battle for Berlin*. New York: Westport, CT: Greenwood, 1996, p. 20.

Chapter Five: How Did the End of World War II Contribute to the Start of the Cold War?

36. Glenn E. Curtis, "The Warsaw Pact," Sam Houston State University. www.shsu.edu.

37. Quoted in Alonzo L. Hamby, "Dealing with Uncle Joe," *Wall Street Journal*, March 14, 2015. www.wsj.com.

38. Quoted in Latin Library, "The Yalta Conference (1945)." www.thelatinlibrary.com.

39. S.M. Plokhy, *Yalta: The Price of Peace*. New York: Viking, 2010, p. 250.

40. Plokhy, *Yalta*, p. 251.

41. Quoted in Richard Overy, *Why the Allies Won*. New York: W.W. Norton, 1997, p. 327.

42. Quoted in Tony Judt, *Postwar: A History of Europe Since 1945*. New York: Penguin, 2005, pp. 106–107.

43. Quoted in *Economist*, "A Conversation with Kennan's Biographer," November 28, 2011. www.economist.com.

44. Richard Reeves, *Daring Young Men: The Heroism and Triumph of the Berlin Airlift, June 1948–May 1949*. New York: Simon & Schuster, 2010, p. xvi.

45. Quoted in Overy, *Why the Allies Won*, p. 329.

Books

Steven M. Gillon, *Pearl Harbor: FDR Leads the Nation into War.* New York: Basic, 2011.

Neil Kagan and Stephen G. Hyslop, *Eyewitness to World War II: Unforgettable Stories and Photographs from History's Greatest Conflict.* Washington DC: National Geographic, 2012.

S.M. Plokhy, *Yalta: The Price of Peace.* New York: Viking, 2010.

Andrew Roberts, *The Storm of War: A New History of the Second World War.* New York: HarperCollins, 2011.

Norman Stone, *World War Two: A Short History.* New York: Basic, 2012.

Internet Sources

Antony Lentin, "Treaty of Versailles: Was Germany Guilty?," *History Today,* January 1, 2012. www.historytoday.com/antony-lentin/treaty-versailles-was-germany-guilty.

Joseph Loconte, "FDR at Yalta: Walking with the Devil," *Weekly Standard,* March 2, 2015. www.weeklystandard.com/blogs/fdr-yalta-walking-devil_871913.html.

Arnold A. Offner, "President Truman and the Origins of the Cold War," BBC, February 17, 2011. www.bbc.co.uk/history/worldwars/wwtwo/truman_01.shtml.

Tom Parfitt, "Vladimir Putin Says There Was Nothing Wrong with Soviet Union's Pact with Adolf Hitler's Nazi Germany," *Telegraph* (London), November 6, 2014. www.telegraph.co.uk/news/worldnews/vladimir-putin/11213255/Vladimir-Putin-says-there-was-nothing-wrong-with-Soviet-Unions-pact-with-Adolf-Hitlers-Nazi-Germany.html.

Alan Taylor, "World War II: Pearl Harbor," *Atlantic,* July 31, 2011. www.theatlantic.com/photo/2011/07/world-war-ii-pearl-harbor/100117/.

Websites

Avalon Project (http://avalon.law.yale.edu). This website features a fascinating collection of documents relating to World War II and its diplomatic background.

The Great War and the Shaping of the 20th Century (http://pbs.org /greatwar). This webpage presents a detailed account of how diplomacy and events at the end of the First World War led to another world war just twenty years later.

History Learning Site (www.historylearningsite.co.uk). This website offers brief, focused articles on World War II, including its causes, major campaigns, weaponry, political leaders, and legacy.

History Place (www.historyplace.com/worldwar2). This website features articles on all aspects of World War II, including detailed accounts, texts of historical documents, and photographs.

WW2History.com (http://ww2history.com). This multimedia website features a library of videos on World War II, including eyewitness accounts of soldiers and civilians. The site also has informative articles on the war, illustrated with photographs from the period.